ABLADE GLOVER

LIGHT & VIBRANCY
PARIS

HANDPICK | JP AKA

ABLADE GLOVER « **Light & Vibrancy Paris** »

Catalogue publiée à l'occasion de la première exposition personnelle de l'artiste à Paris du 14 novembre au 14 décembre 2016.

Exhibition catalogue of the first-ever exhibition of the artists in Paris from November 14 to December 14, 2016.

© HANDPICK | JP AKA

Conception graphique : Marjorie HARROLD
Première édition : Novembre 2016
édité par :
HANDPICK | JP AKA
Paris - Joburg - New York
30, rue de Charonne - 75011 Paris
+33 148072292 | +33 698025383
inquiries@handpickbyjpaka.gallery
www.handpickbyjpaka.gallery

ACKNOWLEDGMENTS / REMERCIEMENTS

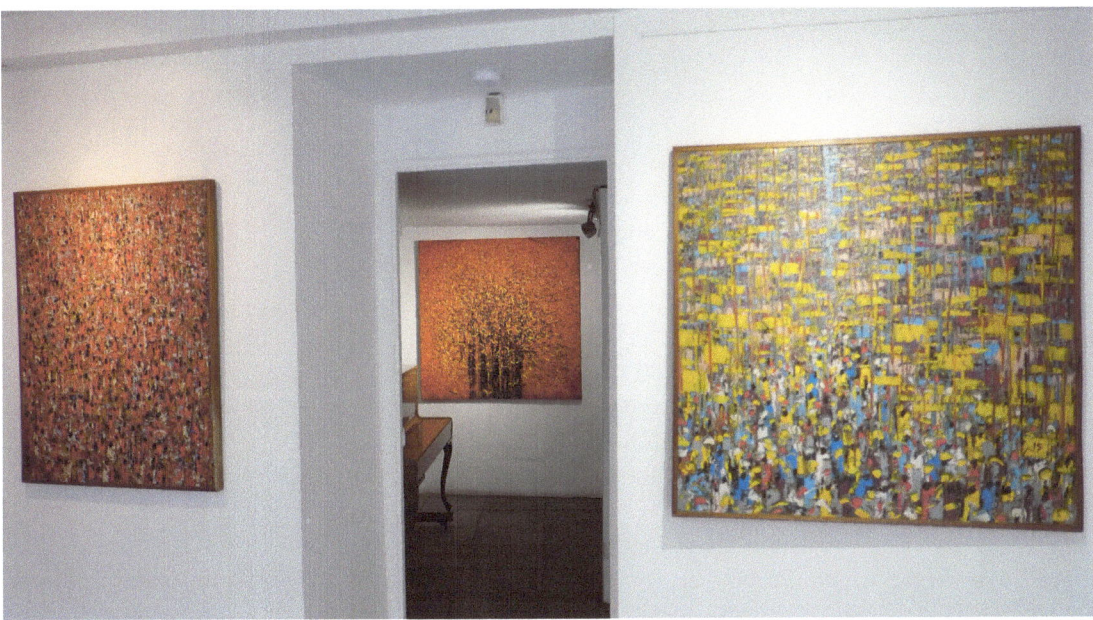

Jean Philippe Aka is grateful to Ms. Simone Guirandou (Louis Simone Guirandou Gallery) for the close collaboration.
Many thanks to Ms. Nicole Louis Sydney for her assistance.

Jean Philippe AKA exprime toute sa gratitude à Simone Guirandou (Louis Simone Guirandou Gallery).
Infiniment merci à Nicole Louis Sydney pour son assistance lors de la préparation de cette exposition.

ABLADE GLOVER
LIGHT AND VIBRANCY PARIS

Ablade Glover is a veteran of Ghana's art scene and one of its most important artists working today. His vibrant paintings depicting local life in Ghana, from scenes of its teeming markets to portaits of its strong women, have been exhibited internationally. The 82-year-old artist has had solo shows in the National Gallery of Modern Art in Lagos, Nigeria, at The Commonwealth Institute in London and at the National Gallery of Zimbabwe, among other locations. Yet his exhibition, Light and Vibrancy in Paris, marks the first time that his work is being honoured with a solo show in France.

As well as being an influential artist, Ablade Glover has played a significant role in the education of art. Having received part of his training in Ghana, Britain and the United States, he was associate professor and head

Ablade Glover est une figure majeure de la scène artistique du Ghana et du continent africain. L'un des artistes en activité parmi les plus importants aujourd'hui. Ses peintures vibrantes représentent la vie locale au Ghana. Ses scènes de marchés grouillants ou ses profils de femmes vaillantes ont été exposés partout dans le monde. L'artiste de 82 ans a eu des expositions personnelles dans des lieux aussi prestigieux que la National Gallery of Modern Art à Lagos, l'Institut du Commonwealth à Londres et au National Gallery du Zimbabwe. Pourtant son exposition *Light & Vibrancy* Paris marque sa première exposition personnelle en France.

En plus d'être un artiste influent, Ablade Glover a joué un rôle important dans l'éducation de l'art. Ayant reçu une partie de sa formation au Ghana, en Grande-Bretagne et aux États-Unis, il a été professeur,chef du département d'éducation artistique et doyen du College of Art à Kwame

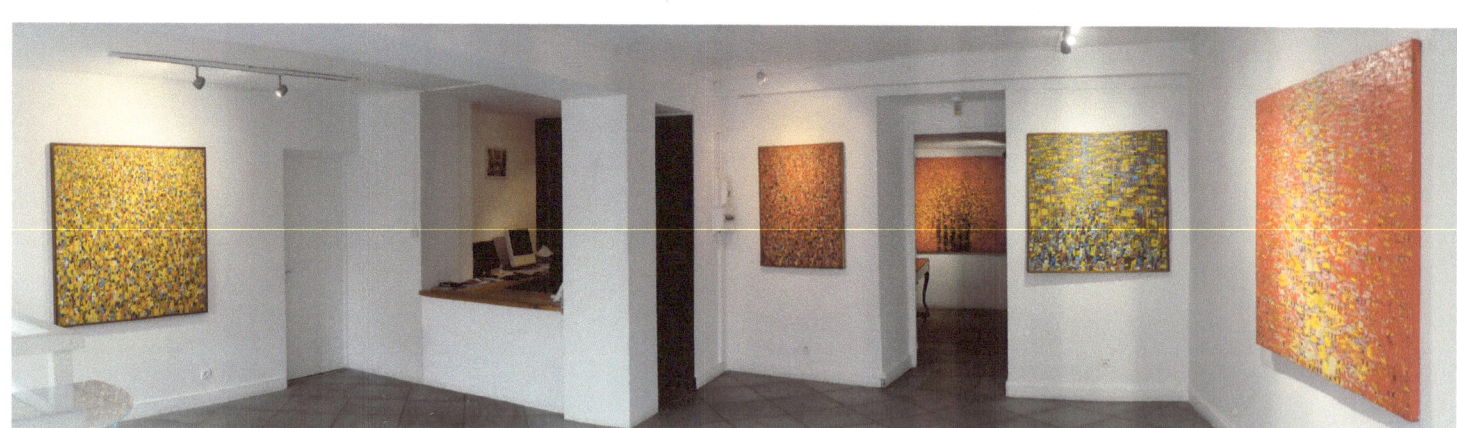

of the department of art education and dean of the College of Art at the Kwame Nkrumah University of Science and Technology in Kumasi. After dedicating himself full-time to art in his later years in Accra, he was awarded the Flagstar Award – Ghana's leading arts award – by the Arts Critics and Reviewers Association of Ghana (ACRAG) in 1998.

This exhibition could have been titled Loving Painting, given how much the love of painting and sharing is felt in each of the works by this icon in the history of contemporary art from Africa. On the cusp of a new era in African art, he is one of the rare few to enjoy recognition both on the stage of the African continent, which is historically centred on local production, and the international stage.

Nkrumah University of Science and Technology de Kumasi. En 1998 pour son engagement dans l'art,il a été récompensé par l'association des critiques artistiques du Ghana (ACRAG).

Cette exposition aurait pu s'intituler *Aimer la peinture* tant peindre et partager se ressent dans chacune des œuvres de cet icône de l'histoire de l'art contemporain africain. À l'orée du vent nouveau qui souffle sur l'art africain, il est un des rares à jouir d'une reconnaissance à la fois sur des scènes continentales, historiquement centrées sur les productions locales, et internationales.

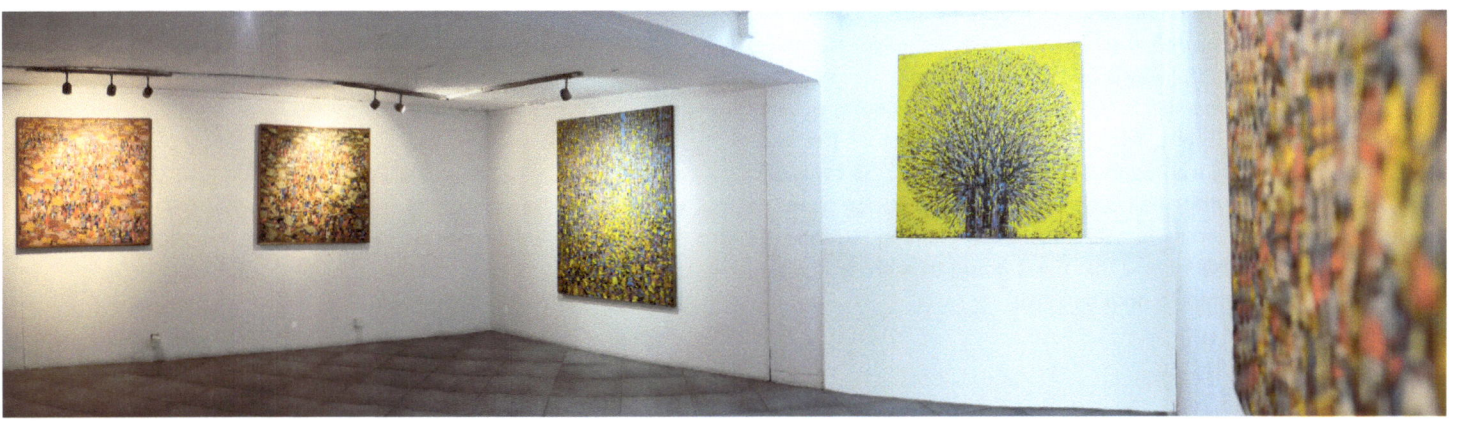

INTERVIEW

Here follows a conversation between the Ghanaian artist Ablade GLOVER and the gallerist Jean-Philippe AKA.

JEAN-PHILIPPE AKA: Do you see yourself as having started as an artist at the end of Africa's modern art period, just before its contemporary art period?

ABLADE GLOVER: African art is a continuum, like a river flowing. In traditional art, artists were expressing themselves in various ways. Then came modern art, followed by our age of contemporary art. You think I was born in the middle but I think that I am in the continuum of what African art is. As a person living in Africa, I am expressing myself. So I do not really see a break-up of the periods of traditional art, modern art and contemporary art. Art historians can begin to see people belonging to a certain period, but I see myself in a continuum.

JPA: How did you become an artist?

AG: I didn't start out as an artist. I wanted to be a teacher and through teaching I found that I excelled in art. So I became an art teacher. I discovered the work of Saka Acquaye. He had a beautiful way of portraying Ghanaian womanhood, he was like a role model for me. Painting became my hobby. With teaching, I had a lot of free time and I wanted to do what I loved most. So I was half painting, half lecturing. But since retiring from the university in 1993, I've been painting full time. By 1990, I knew that I was going to retire and what I wanted to do afterwards.

Conversation entre l'artiste Ablade GLOVER et le galeriste Jean-Philippe AKA

JEAN-PHILIPPE AKA : Au regard de l'histoire vous définissez-vous comme celui qui clôt le modernisme et annonce la période contemporaine ?

ABLADE GLOVER : L'art africain est un continuum, comme une rivière qui coule. Dans l'art traditionnel, les artistes s'exprimaient de diverses manières. Puis est venu l'art moderne, suivi par notre temps de l'art contemporain. Vous me situez par rapport à cette période, mais je pense que je suis dans le continuum de ce qu'est l'art africain. En tant que personne vivant en Afrique, je m'exprime. Je ne vois donc pas vraiment une rupture des périodes de l'art traditionnel, de l'art moderne et de l'art contemporain. Les historiens de l'art peuvent commencer à voir des personnes appartenant à une certaine période, mais je me vois dans un continuum.

JPA : Comment êtes-vous arrivé à la peinture ?

AG : Je n'ai pas commencé comme artiste. Je voulais être un enseignant et grâce à l'enseignement, j'ai trouvé ma voie dans l'art. Je suis devenu professeur d'art. J'ai découvert le travail de Saka Acquaye. Il avait une belle façon de représenter la féminité ghanéenne, il était comme un modèle pour moi. La peinture est devenue mon hobby. Avec l'enseignement, j'ai eu beaucoup de temps libre et je voulais faire ce que j'aimais le plus. Donc, j'étais à moitié peintre, à moitié enseignant. Mais depuis ma retraite de l'université en 1993, je peins à temps plein. Dès 1990, je savais que j'allais prendre ma retraite et je savais ce que je voulais faire par la suite.

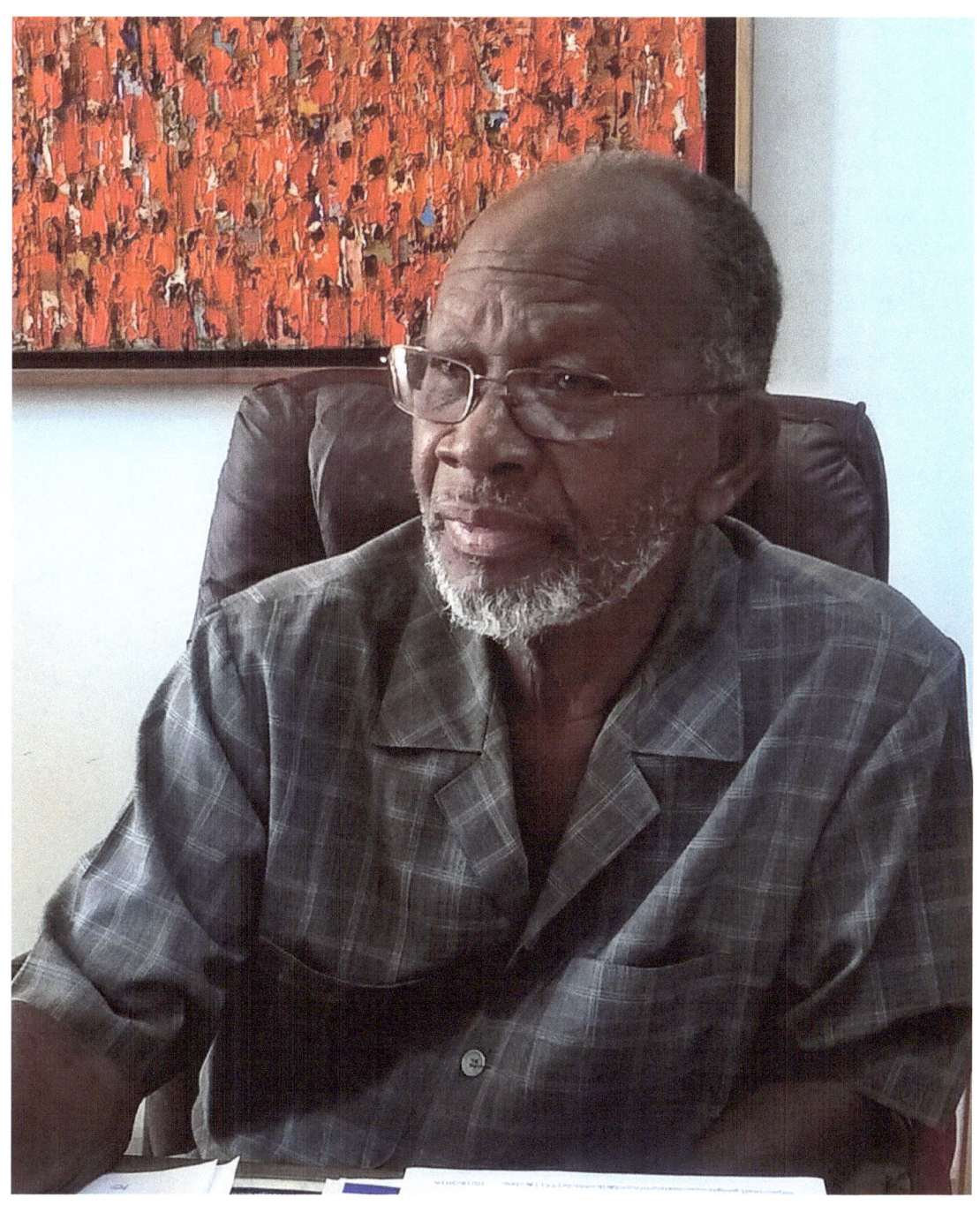

JPA: What captures your imagination and motivates you to paint?

AG: I feel that Ghana is a very vibrant and dynamic society. Society is not standing still. I see a lot of women around me in the market, people are moving all the time, and the colours are beautiful. This is all fascinating and captures my imagination. I paint people, I paint the market, I paint the flowers. I want to make people aware of the vibrancy, the strength and the beauty of life in Ghana. You have to put it onto canvas to convey the feeling. This is what I try to capture.

JPA: I've noticed that there are only a few abstract painters in Africa. Would you agree with that?

AG: Yes, in contemporary art, I would agree with that. At the moment, there is not much attention on abstract art. But abstract art must depend on something; it is not depending on a vacuum. Abstract art comes from realistic living, from life. If someone is painting abstract art, it is not abstract at all. Some people say that I'm painting abstract art. But I'm not painting abstract art at all. I'm struggling to convey a story that this nation is beautiful, vibrant and strong, not dormant or dying. It is a great society that is alive and well. Conveying that is what I'm trying to do.

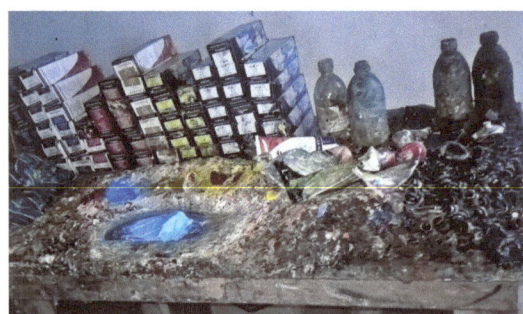

JPA: What does the human figure represent for you?

AG: My paintings tell a story about the female figures around us. The male figure disappoints me, I must say, but the female figure is amazing. Look at the women in the market: they get up early in the morning and go to work. Their positive attitude and strength is what I'm portraying. In spite of centuries of slavery taking place in Africa, this culture didn't die. So I don't know what could kill our culture, because slavery did take place and was like a genocide.

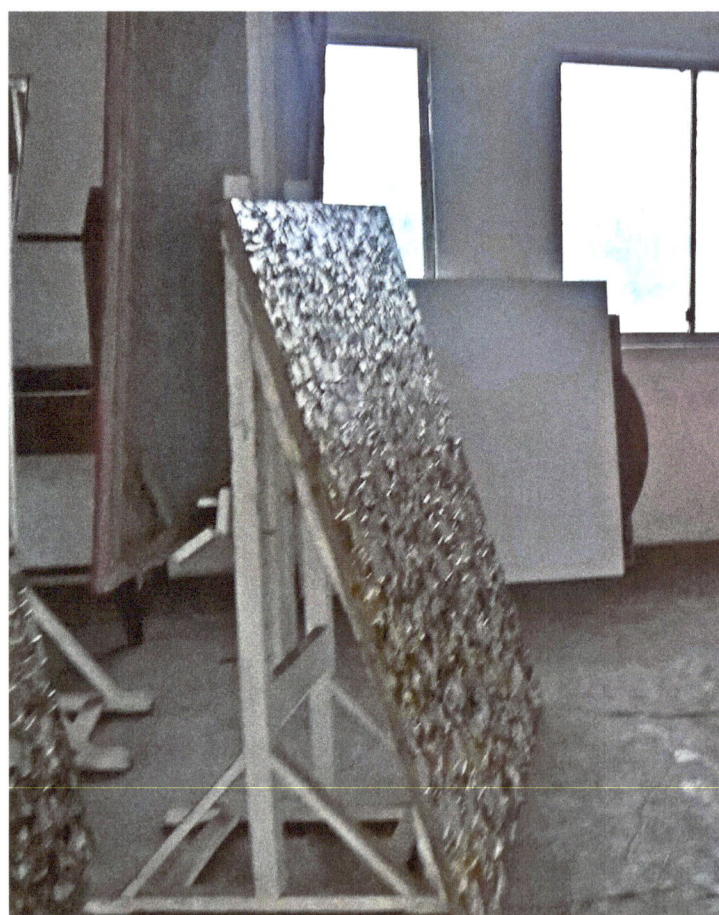

JPA : Quelles sont vos sources d'inspirations ?

AG : Je pense que le Ghana est une société en mouvement, dynamique. La société n'est pas immobile. Je vois beaucoup de femmes autour de moi sur le marché, les gens se déplacent tout le temps, et les couleurs sont belles. Tout cela est fascinant et capte mon imagination. Je peins les gens, je peins le marché, je peins les fleurs. Je veux sensibiliser les gens au dynamisme, à la force et à la beauté de la vie au Ghana. Mettre tout cela sur la toile pour transmettre le sentiment. C'est ce que j'essaie de capturer.

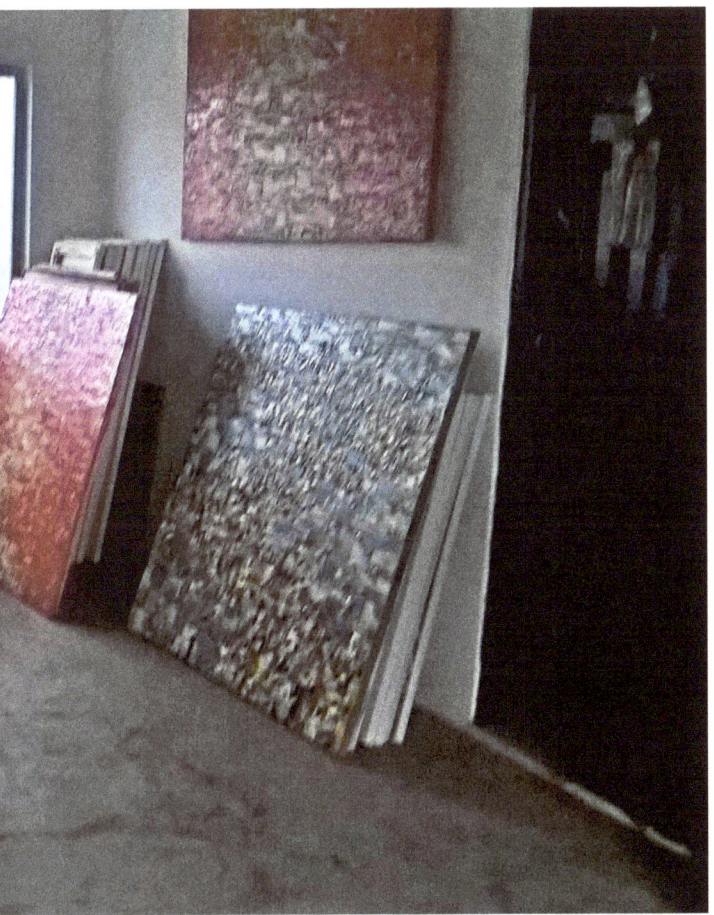

JPA : Tout au long du XXᵉ siècle en Afrique, on remarque qu'il y a peu d'artistes qui s'adonnent à l'abstraction. Partagez-vous cet avis ?

AG : Oui, dans l'art contemporain, je suis d'accord. À l'heure actuelle, on n'accorde pas beaucoup d'attention à l'art abstrait. Mais l'art abstrait doit provenir de quelque chose ; il ne provient pas d'un vide. L'art abstrait vient de la vie réelle, de la vie. Si quelqu'un peint de l'art abstrait, il n'est pas du tout abstrait. Certaines personnes disent que je peins l'art abstrait. Mais je ne peins pas l'art abstrait du tout. Je lutte pour transmettre une histoire, que cette Nation est belle, dynamique et forte, non dormante ou mourante. C'est une grande société qui est vivante et bien. Transposer tout ça, c'est ce que j'essaie de faire.

JPA : La représentation de la figure humaine est-elle une préoccupation dans votre peinture ?

AG : Mes tableaux racontent une histoire sur les personnages féminins qui nous entourent. La figure masculine me déçoit, je dois dire, mais la figure féminine est étonnante. Regardez les femmes sur le marché : elles se lèvent tôt le matin pour aller au travail. Leur attitude positive et leur force sont ce que je dépeins. Malgré des siècles d'esclavage en Afrique, cette culture n'est pas morte. Donc je ne sais pas ce qui pourrait tuer notre culture, après l'esclavage qui était comme un génocide.

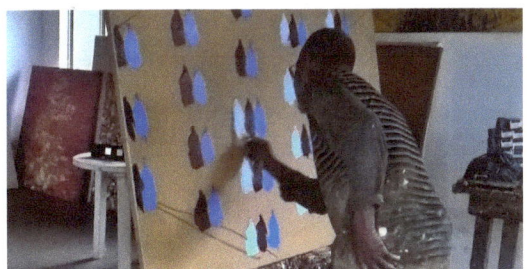

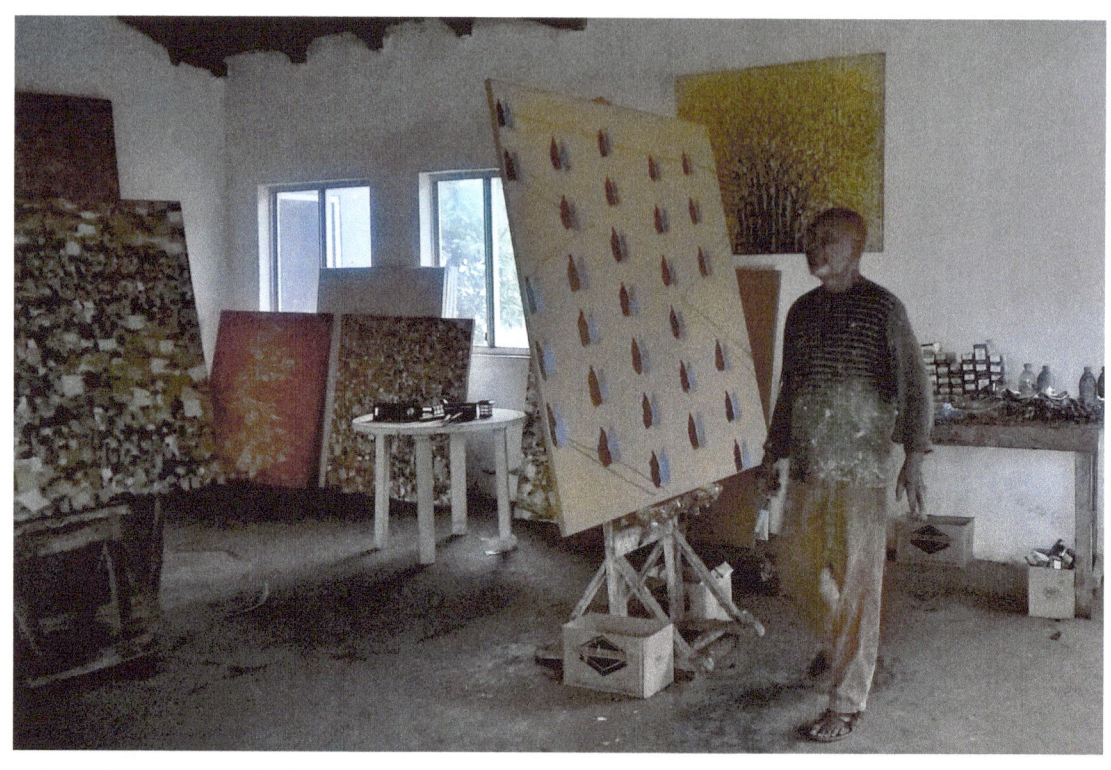

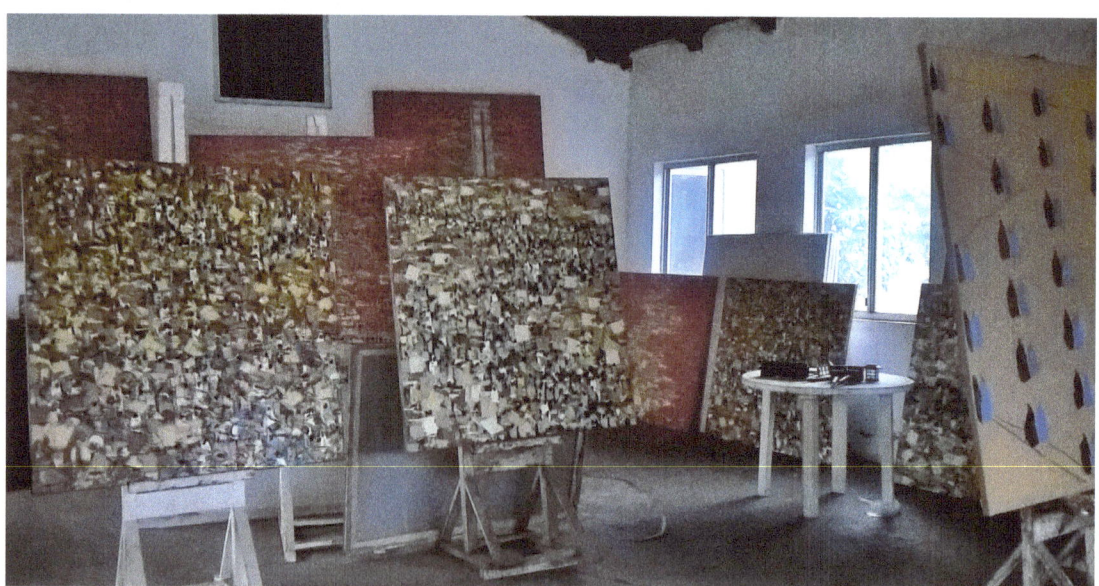

JPA: Are there any particular works of literature that have been inspirational for you?

AG: Not really. I haven't read much; I'm not much of a literary scholar. What has influenced me is people who have conveyed their messages in visual form. I mentioned Saka Acquaye, whose female figures I still try to study.

JPA: When did you establish your studio?

AG: I've always had a studio. When I was in Kumasi, I used my bungalow on the campus as my studio and had my paintbrushes there. When I returned to Accra, I built my own house and built a studio attached to it, a little further along. I get up in the morning and walk to the studio with a cup of tea. I need to have a studio around me all the time, wherever I am, because you never know when you'll feel like painting. Painting for me is like writing for a writer: you're sitting somewhere and an idea comes. Whenever I'm somewhere for a few hours, I build a studio around me as part of my living area.

JPA: How would you describe a day in your studio?

AG: In the morning, I go to the studio and usually I already have a canvas standing on the easel. That means I had an idea the day before and knew what I was going to do. I'd been dreaming about something – maybe a market, maybe some women walking, maybe a profile. It's like a dream, I dream that I'm going to paint this crowd, or this celebration, whatever this celebration is. Sometimes I sketch before I start painting but most of the time I don't sketch at all. The most important thing is to take myself into the studio. When I'm in the studio, things begin to emerge. It's a great, crazy feeling that's hard to describe. But I go on to do something with the day.

JPA : La littérature vous inspire-t-elle dans votre travail ?

AG : Pas vraiment. Je n'ai pas lu beaucoup ; je ne suis pas un savant littéraire. Ce qui m'a influencé, ce sont les gens qui m'ont transmis leurs messages sous forme visuelle. J'ai parlé de Saka Acquaye, dont je cherche toujours à étudier les personnages féminins.

JPA : Parlez-moi de votre atelier ?

AG : J'ai toujours eu un atelier. Quand j'étais à Kumasi, j'ai utilisé mon bungalow sur le campus comme mon studio et j'avais mes pinceaux là. Quand je suis retourné à Accra, j'ai construit ma propre maison et un studio, un peu plus loin.
Je me lève le matin et je marche vers mon atelier avec une tasse de thé. J'ai besoin d'avoir un atelier autour de moi tout le temps, où que je sois, parce que je ne sais jamais quand j'aurai envie de peindre. La peinture pour moi est comme écrire pour un écrivain : assis quelque part et une idée vient. Chaque fois que je suis quelque part pour quelques heures, je m'arrange pour avoir un atelier.

JPA : Comment décrirez-vous une journée dans votre atelier ?

Le matin, je vais au studio et habituellement j'ai déjà une toile debout sur le chevalet. Cela signifie que j'ai eu une idée la veille et savais ce que j'allais faire. J'avais rêvé de quelque chose - peut-être un marché, peut-être des femmes marchant, peut-être un profil. C'est comme un rêve, je rêve que je vais peindre cette foule ou cette célébration, quelle que soit cette célébration. Parfois, je dessine avant de commencer à peindre, mais la plupart du temps je ne dessine pas du tout. La chose la plus importante est de me retrouver dans l'atelier. Une fois que j'y suis, les choses commencent à émerger. C'est un intense sentiment, qui est difficile à décrire. Mais je vais faire quelque chose avec la journée.

JPA: What is the importance of the palette knife in your work?

AG: The palette knife is a great tool because you can scrape the paint off the canvas immediately. Therefore it gives you the freedom to go and come back and do it again. Then after using the palette knife, the figure begins to emerge. It was a teacher in Newcastle, where I was teaching in the mid-1960s, who advised me to use the palette knife. He said, *"Hey, if you use a palette knife, you will be better off."* And he was right because I can thrash the canvas with the palette knife and it has been life-saving!

JPA: How do you feel about having this exhibition in Paris?

AG: I've never been to Paris because I've never had the opportunity or the courage to visit the city. I know it's a great city in the history of art. Van Gogh is the number one artist for me and I hope I will see some of his work when I come over for my exhibition. ∎

JPA : Vous être passé maître dans la technique au couteau que vous avez adoptez il y a un peu plus de 50 ans.

Le couteau est un excellent outil car vous pouvez gratter la peinture sur la toile immédiatement. Par conséquent, il vous donne la liberté d'aller et de revenir et de le faire à nouveau. Ensuite, après avoir utilisé la technique au couteau, la figure commence à émerger. C'était un professeur à Newcastle, où j'enseignais au milieu des années 1960, qui m'a conseillé d'utiliser le couteau à palette.
Il a dit : « *Si vous utilisez la technique au couteau, vous serez mieux* ». Et il avait raison parce que j'ai pu ainsi m'approprier la toile avec cette technique et ça m'a sauvé la vie !

JPA : Je suis plus qu'honoré de présenter votre première exposition personnelle à Paris c'est un cadeau !

Je n'ai jamais été à Paris parce que je n'ai jamais eu l'occasion ou le courage de visiter la ville. Je sais que c'est une grande ville dans l'histoire de l'art. Van Gogh est l'artiste numéro un pour moi et j'espère que je vais voir un peu de son travail quand je viens pour mon exposition. ∎

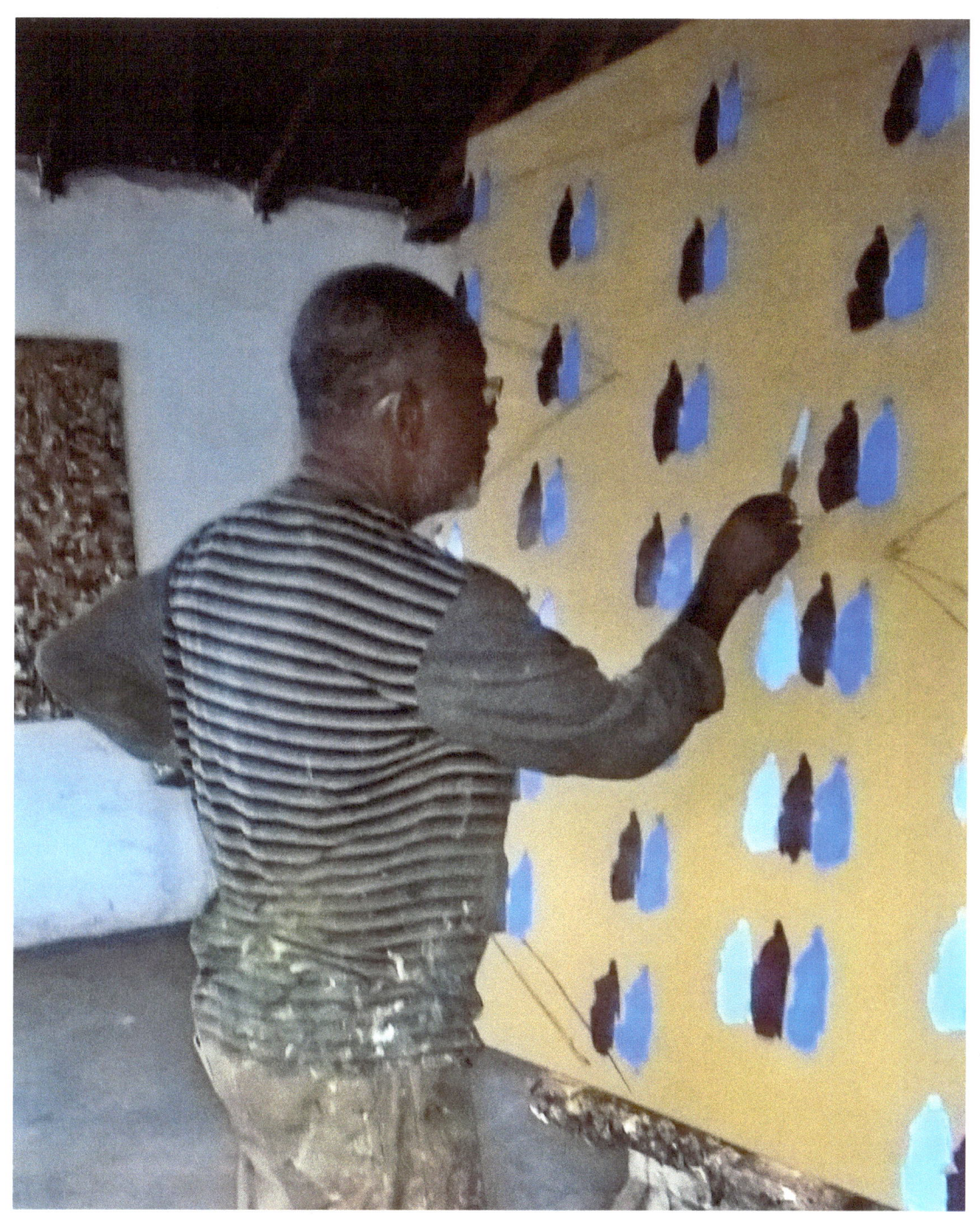

–

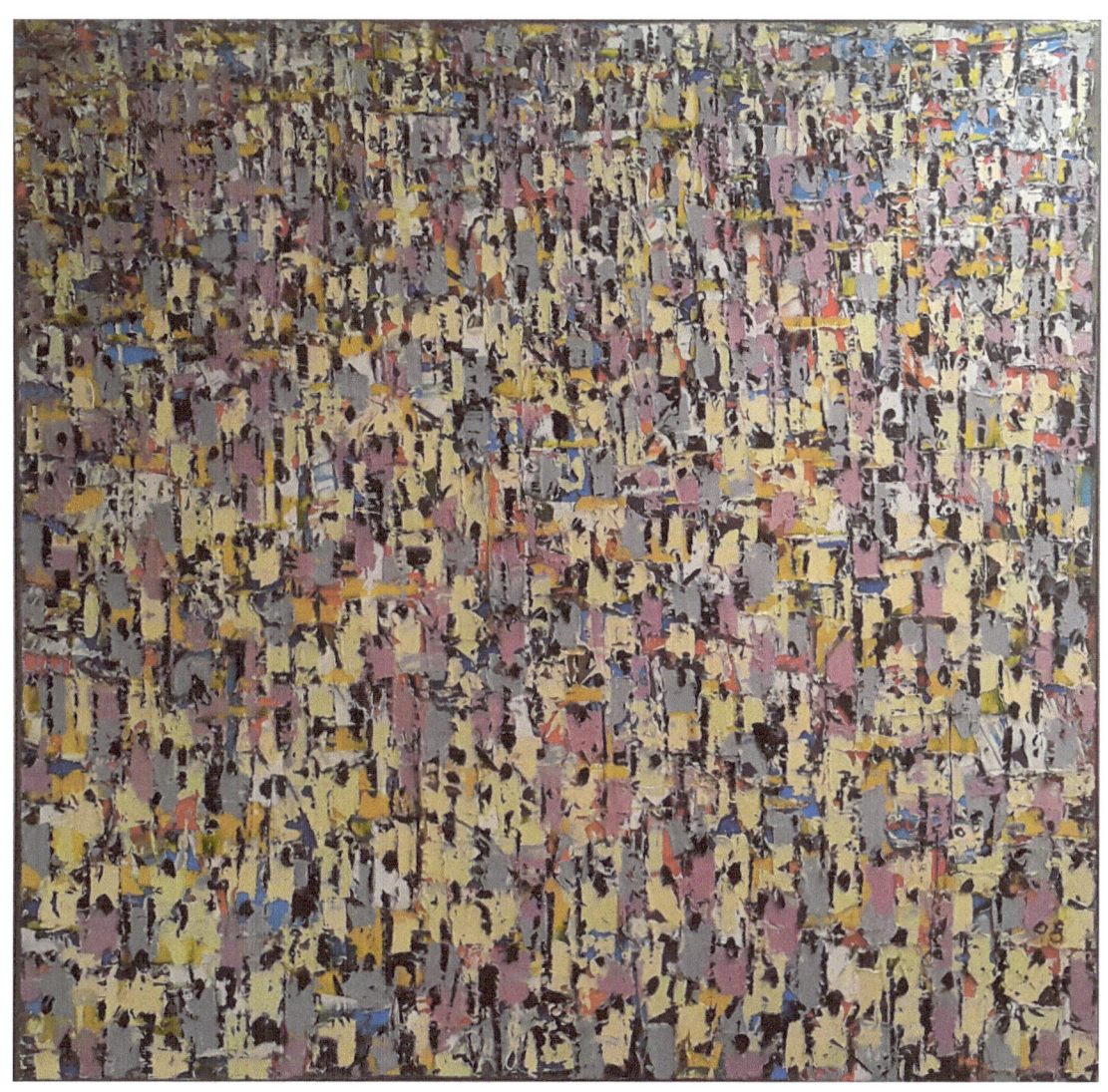

Prayers, 2008, huile sur toile - 150 x 100 cm coll. privée Joburg

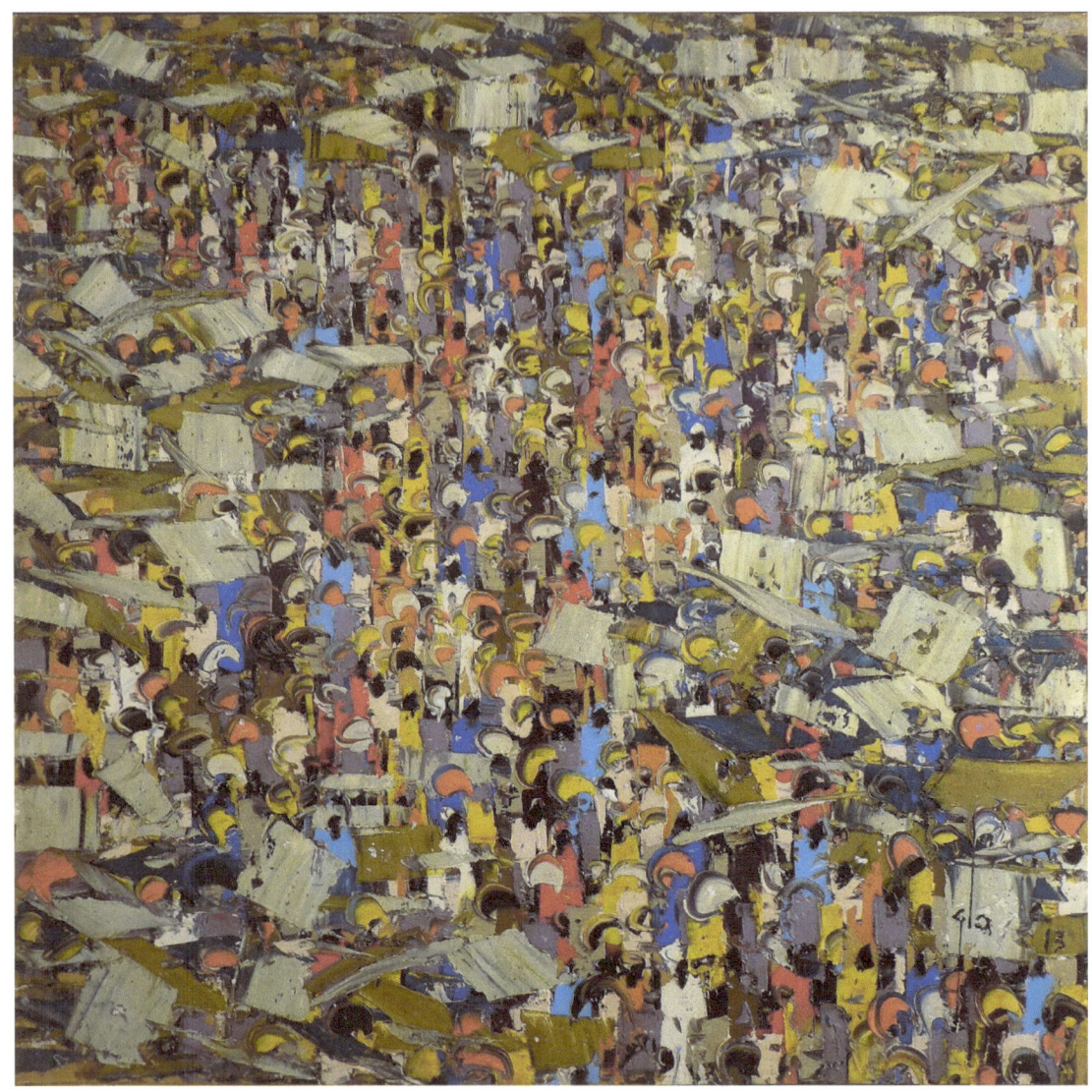

Carnival, 2013, huile sur toile - 100 x 100 cm

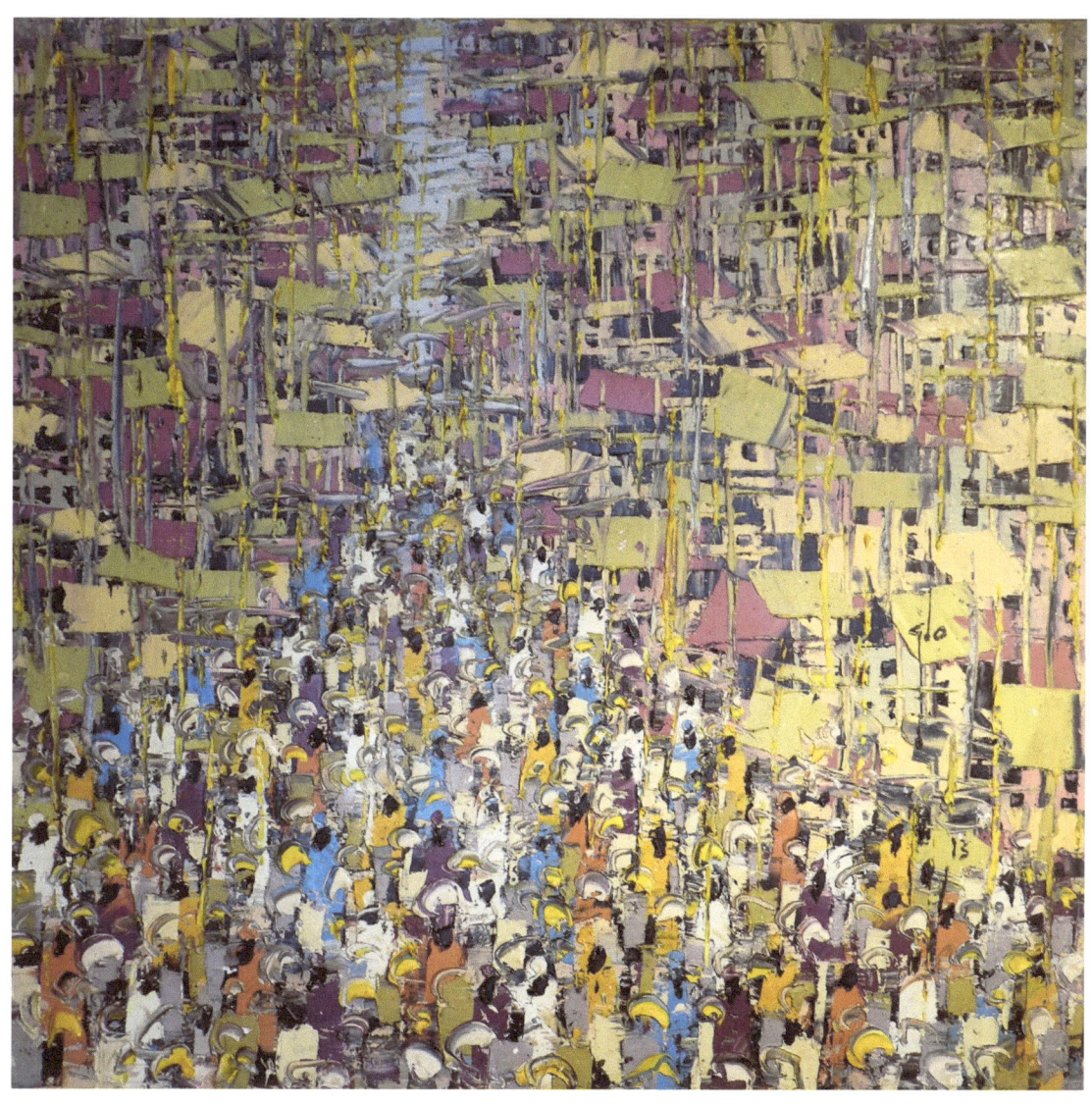

Jubilation, 2013, huile sur toile - 100 x 100 cm

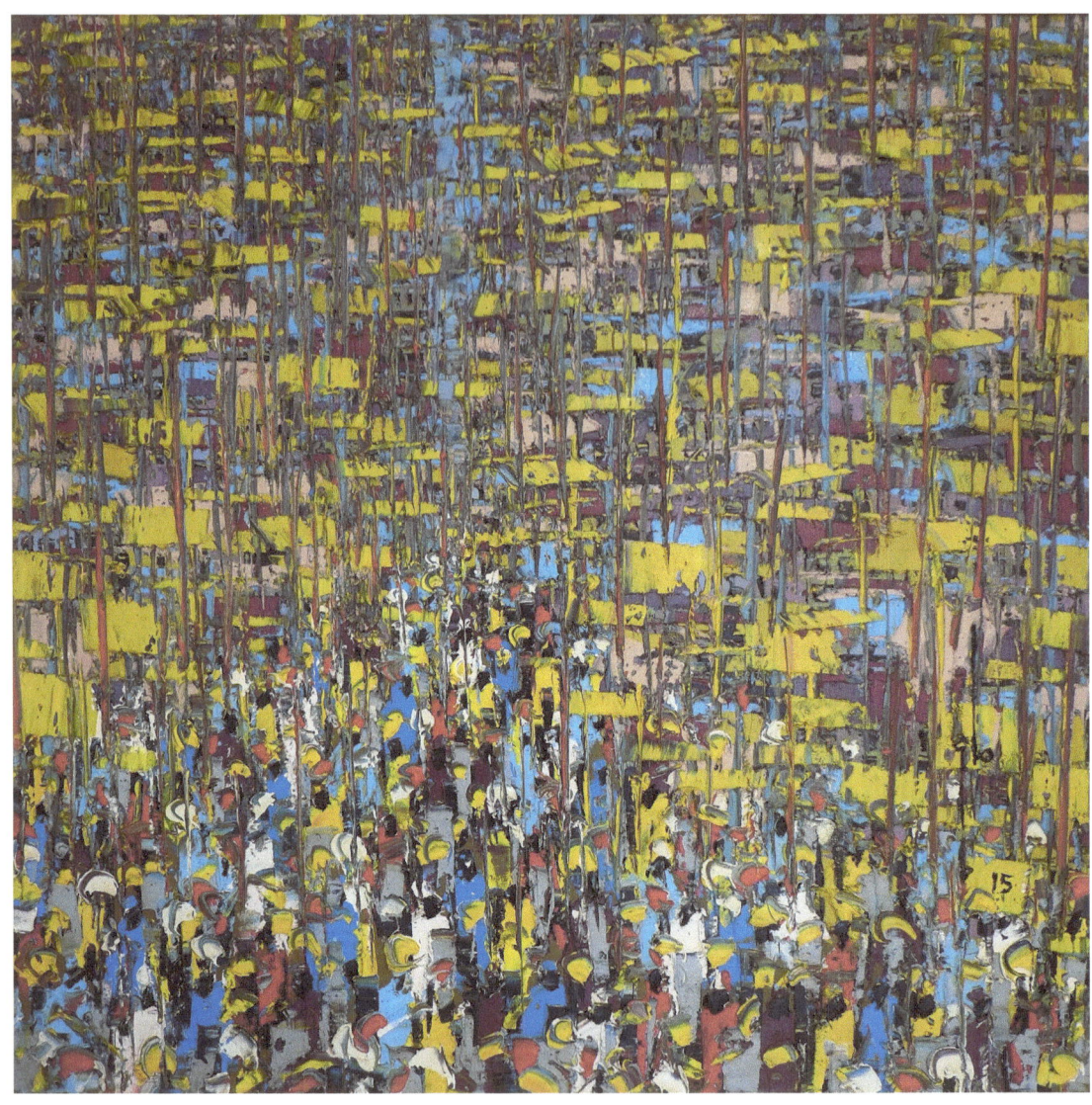

Jubilation, 2015, huile sur toile - 100 x 100 cm

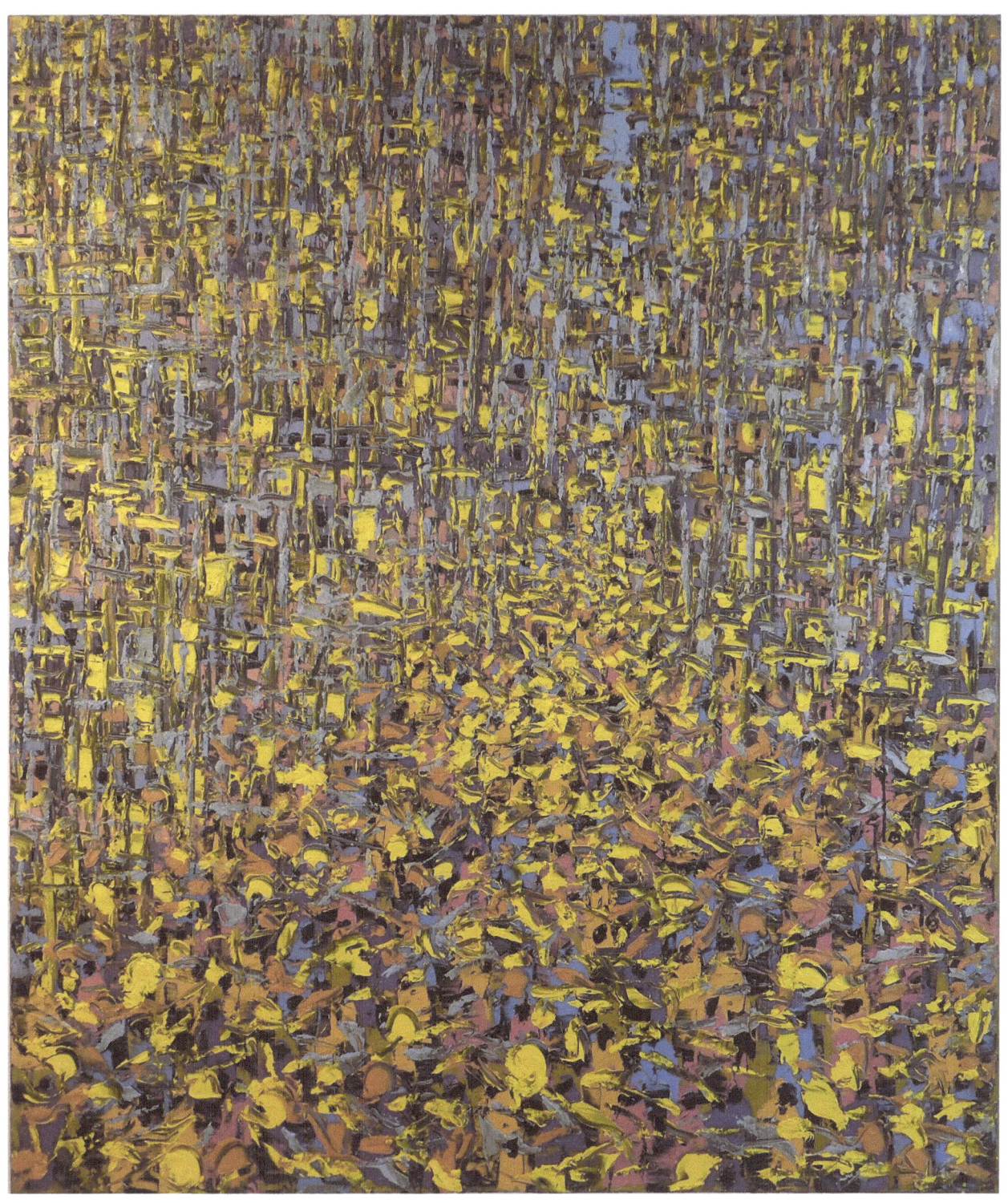

Jubilation, 2016, huile sur toile - 122 x 152 cm

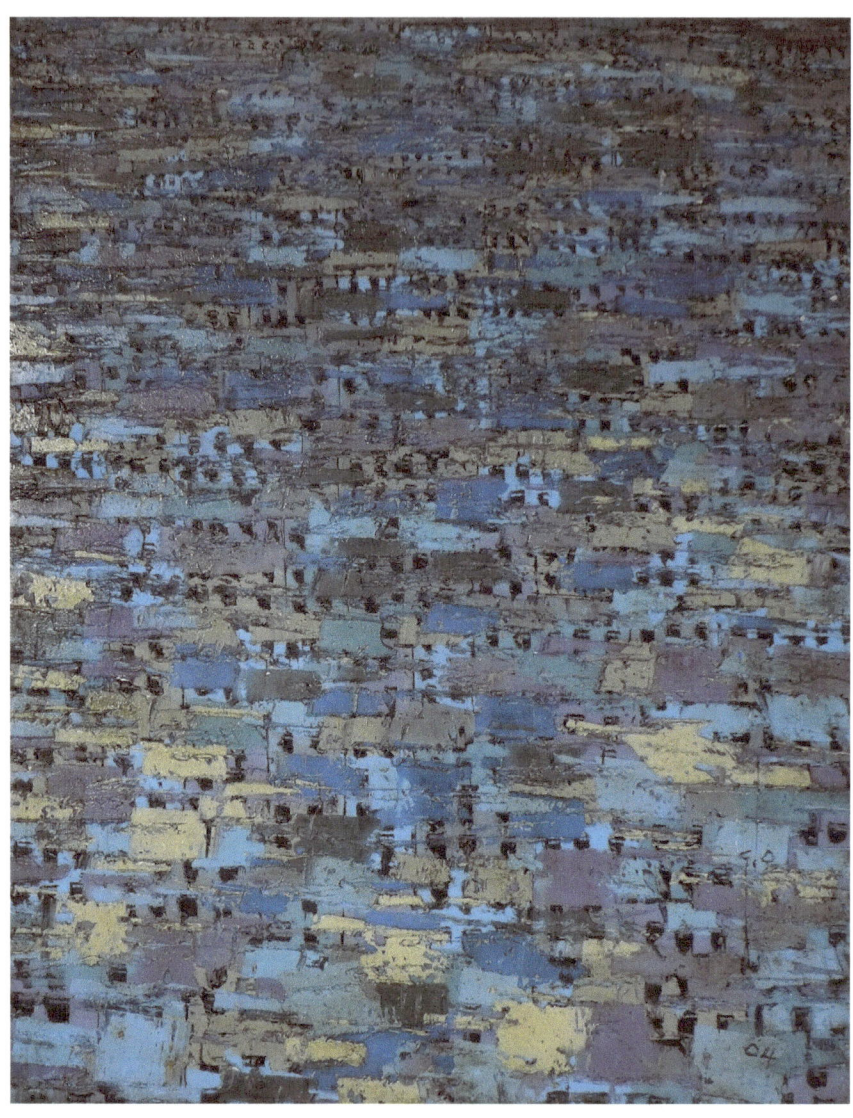

Day Break, 2004, huile sur toile - 76 x 100 cm

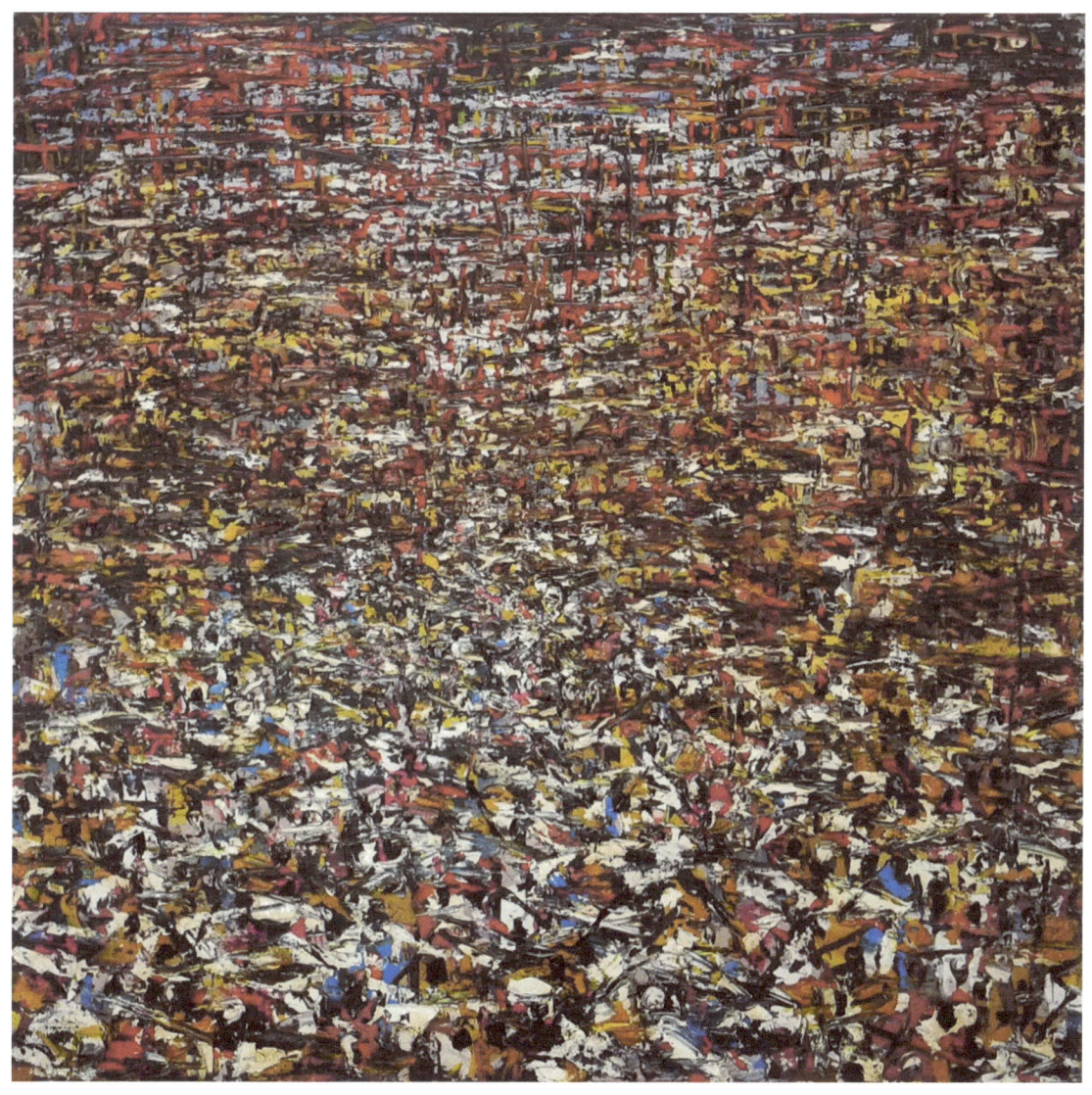

Market Lane, 2013, huile sur toile - 100 x 100 cm

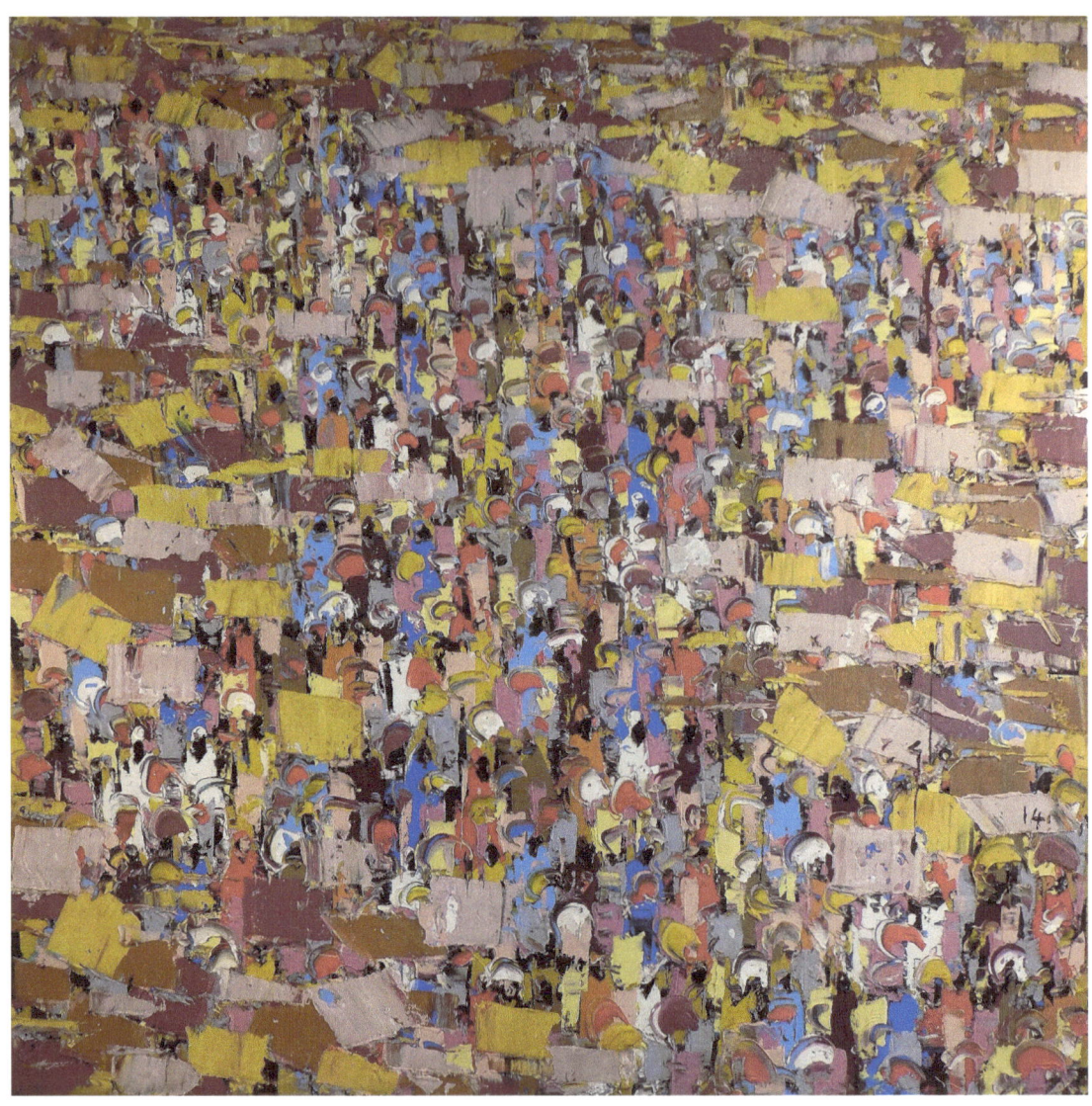

Market Lane, 2014, huile sur toile - 100 x 100 cm

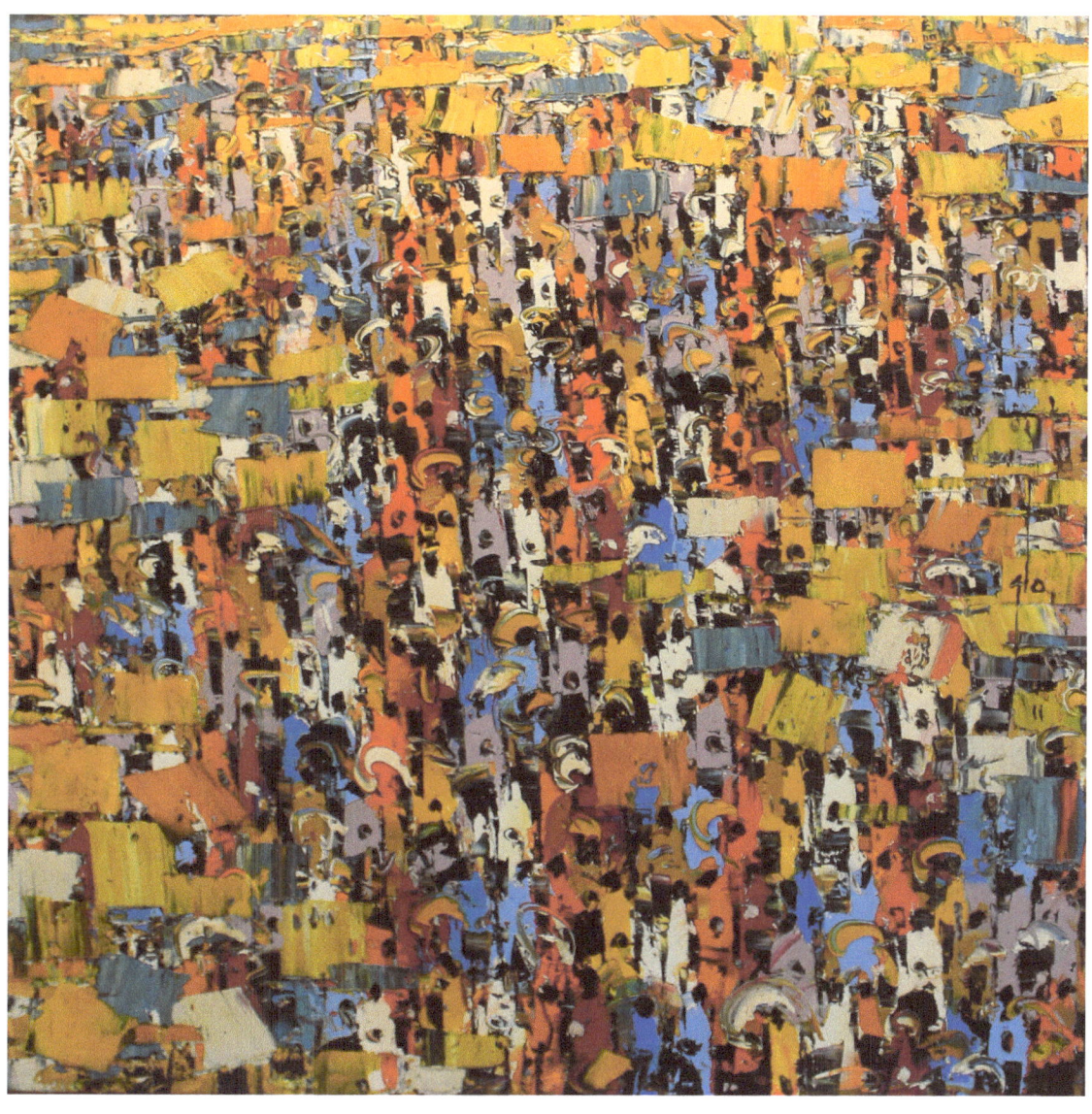

Market Lane, 2011, huile sur toile - 100 x 100 cm coll. privée Paris

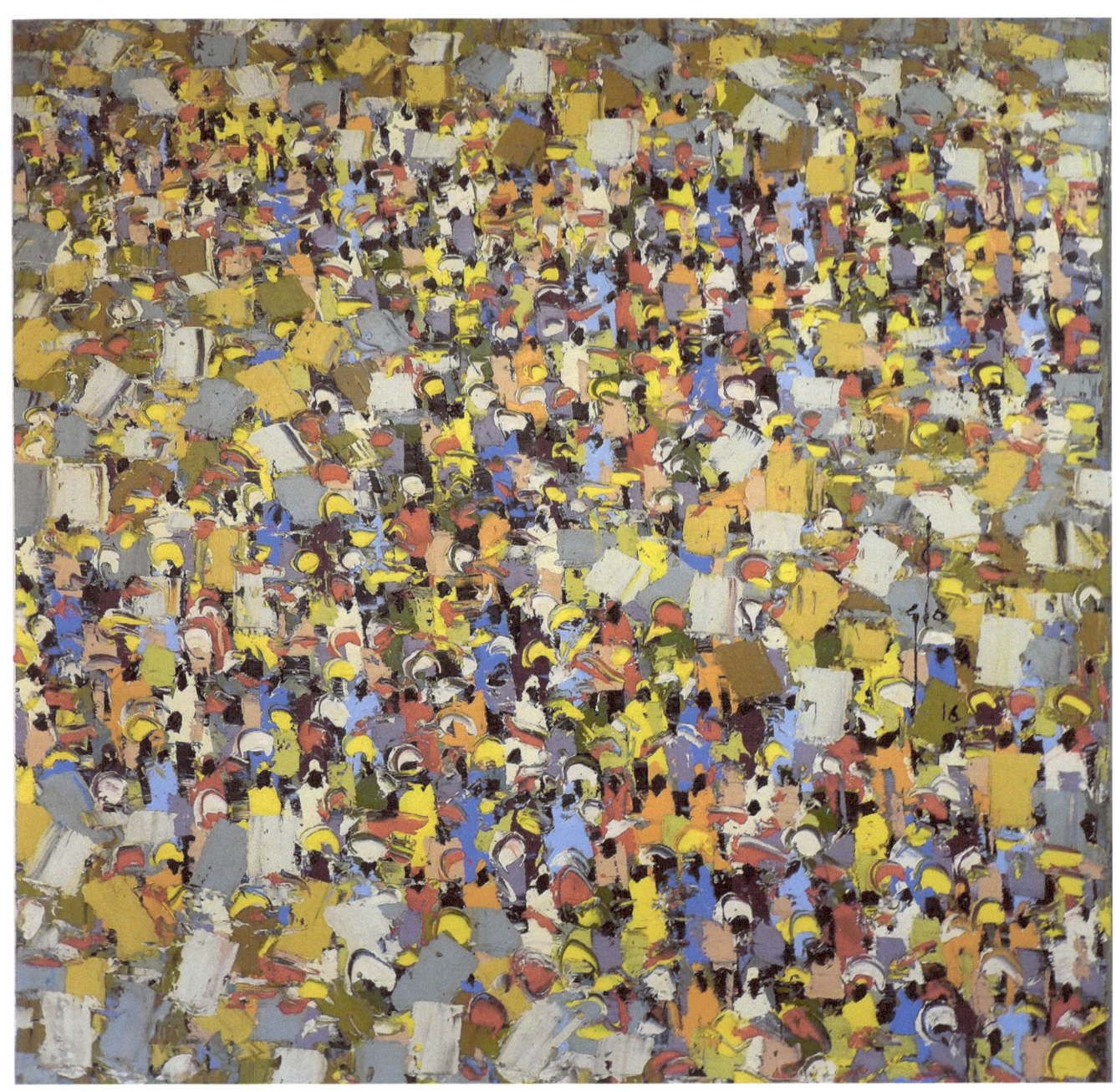

Marketscape, 2016, huile sur toile - 122 x 122 cm

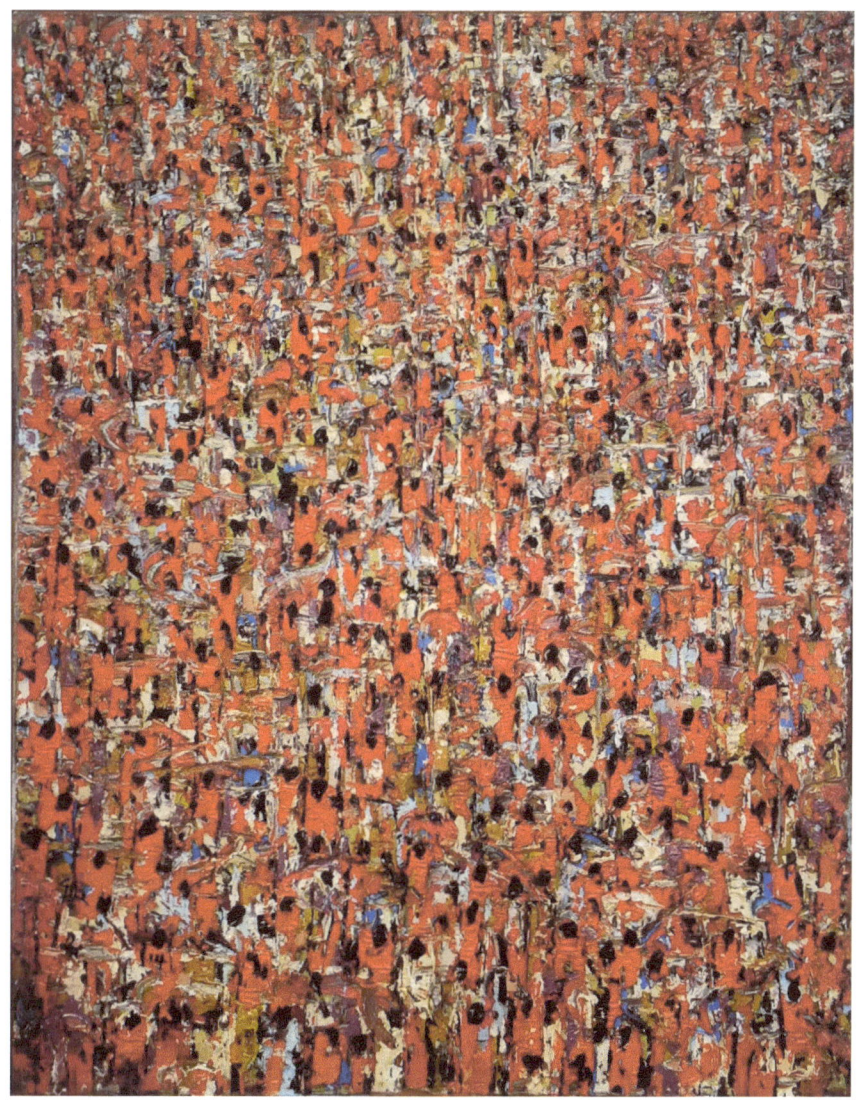

People, 2014 huile sur toile, 76 x 100 cm coll. privée Paris

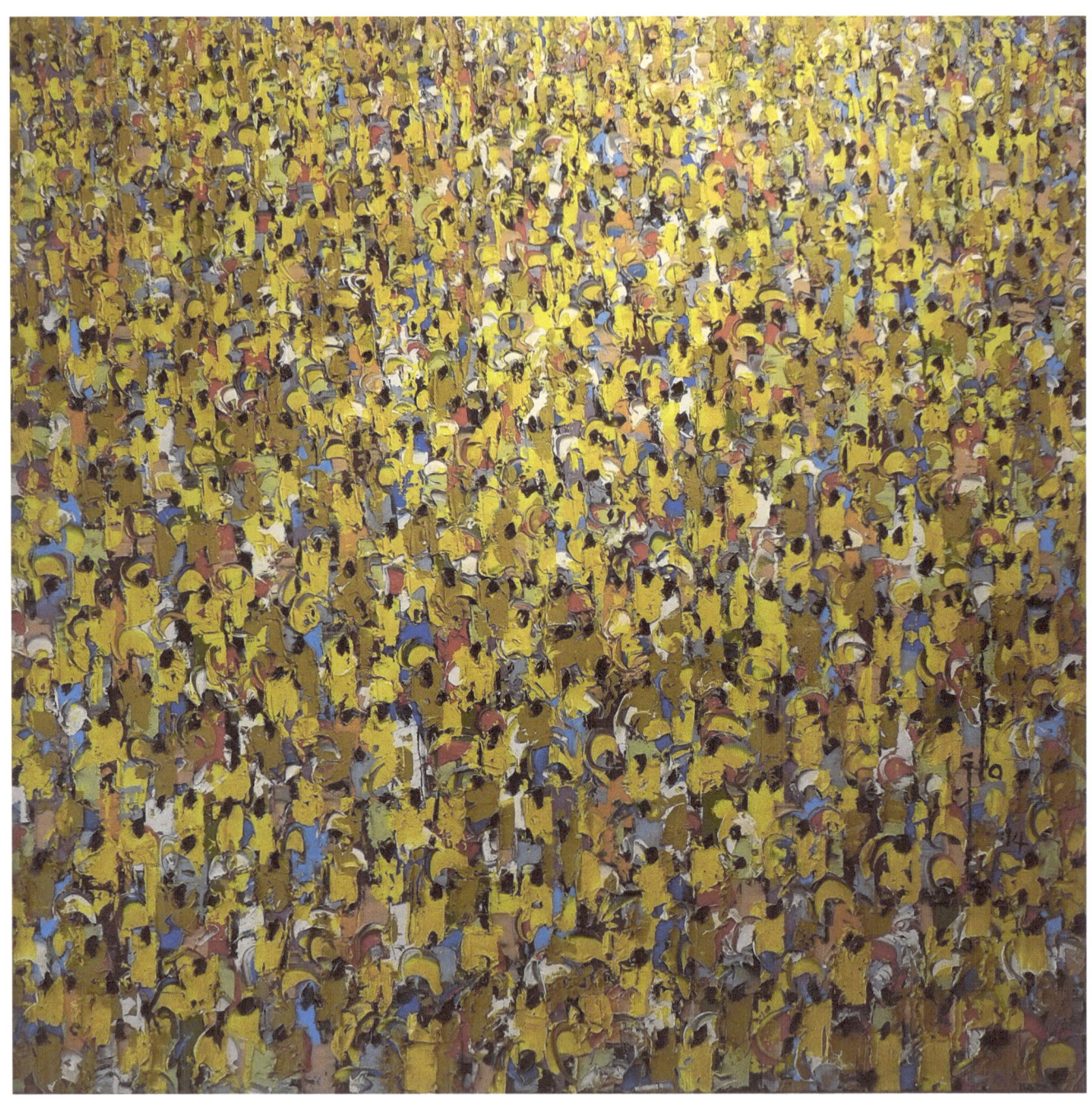

People, 2014, huile sur toile - 120 x 120 cm

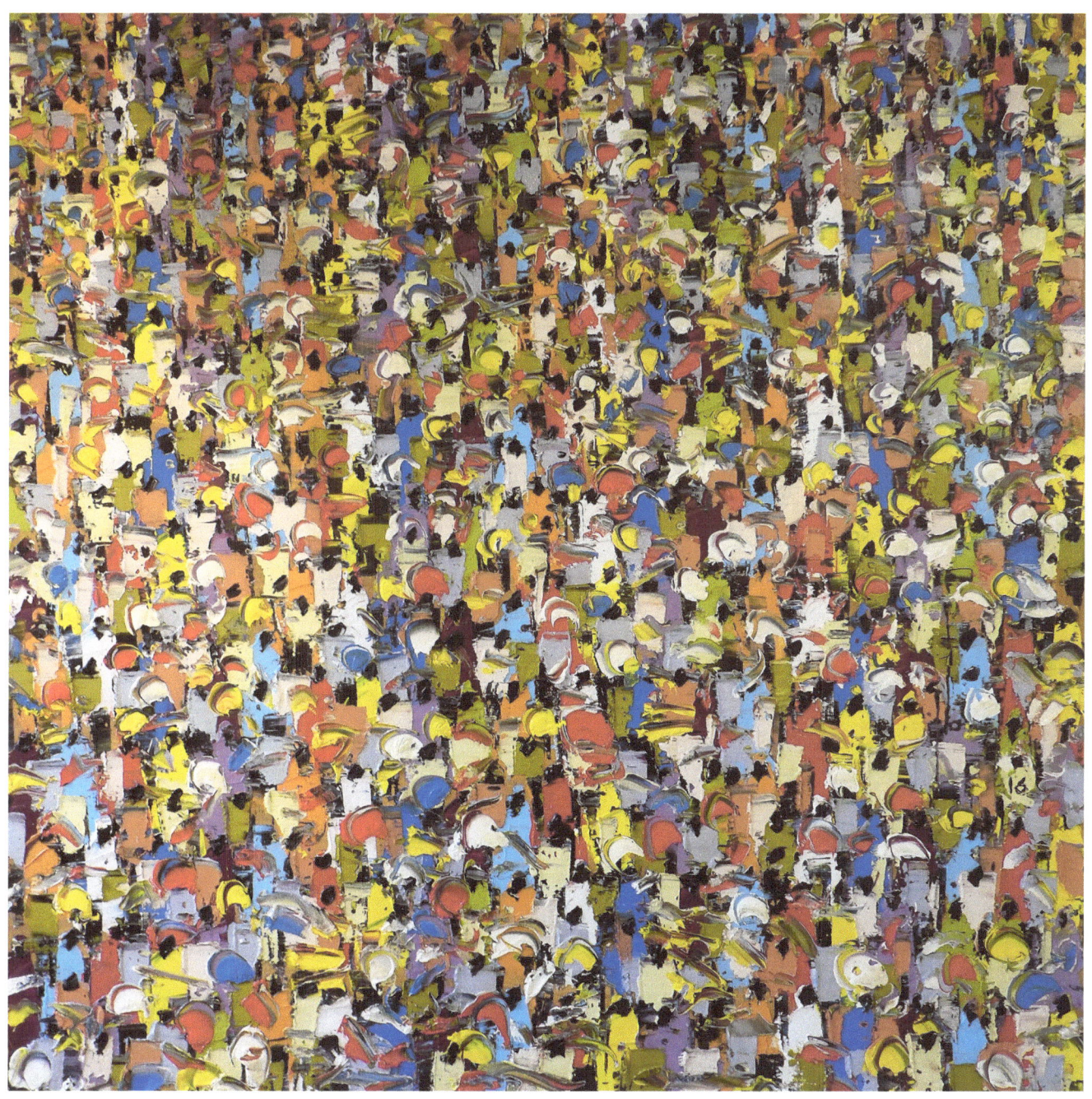

People, 2016, huile sur toile - 122 x 122 cm

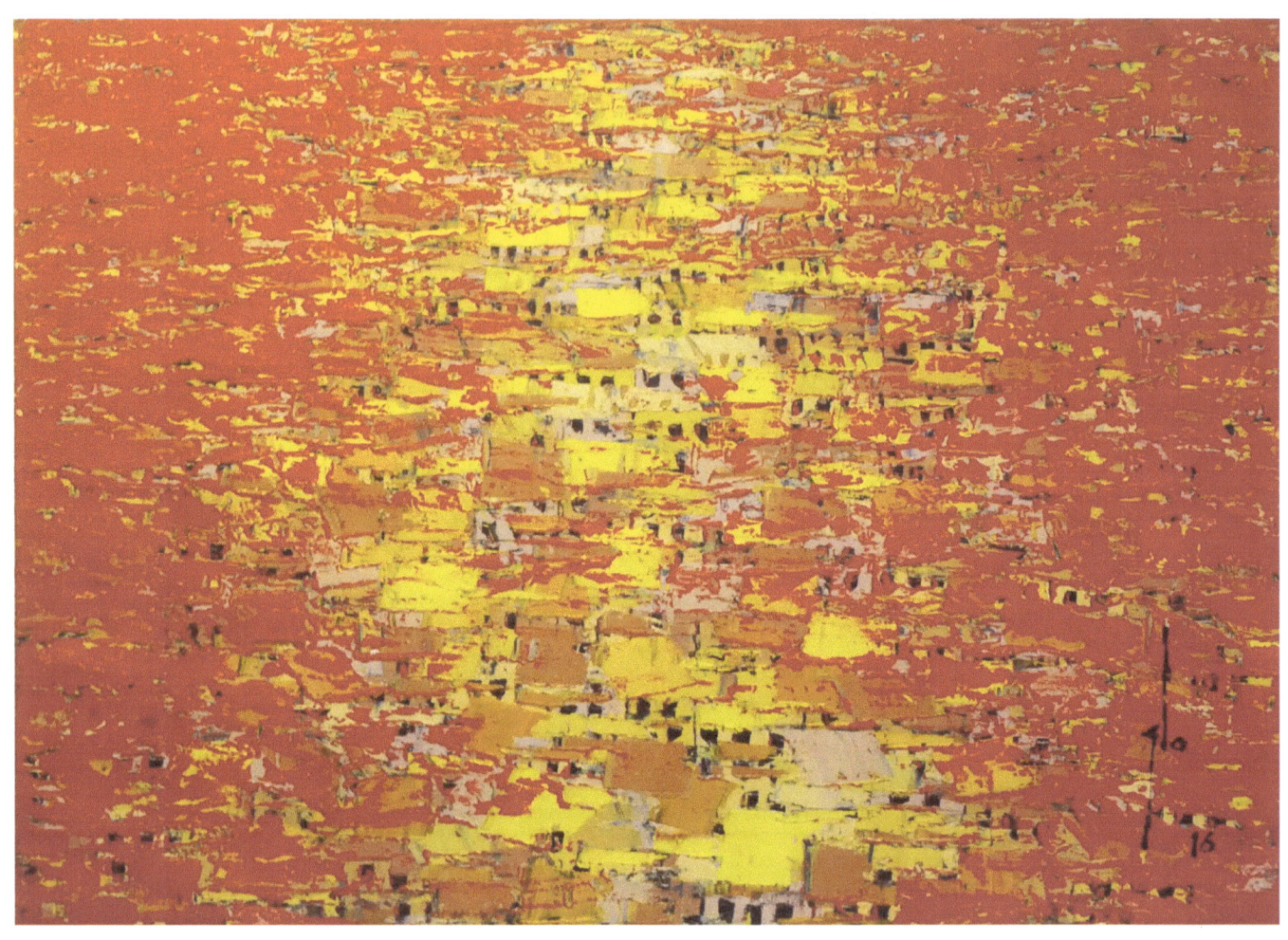

Red townscape, 2016, huile sur toile - 102 x 127 cm

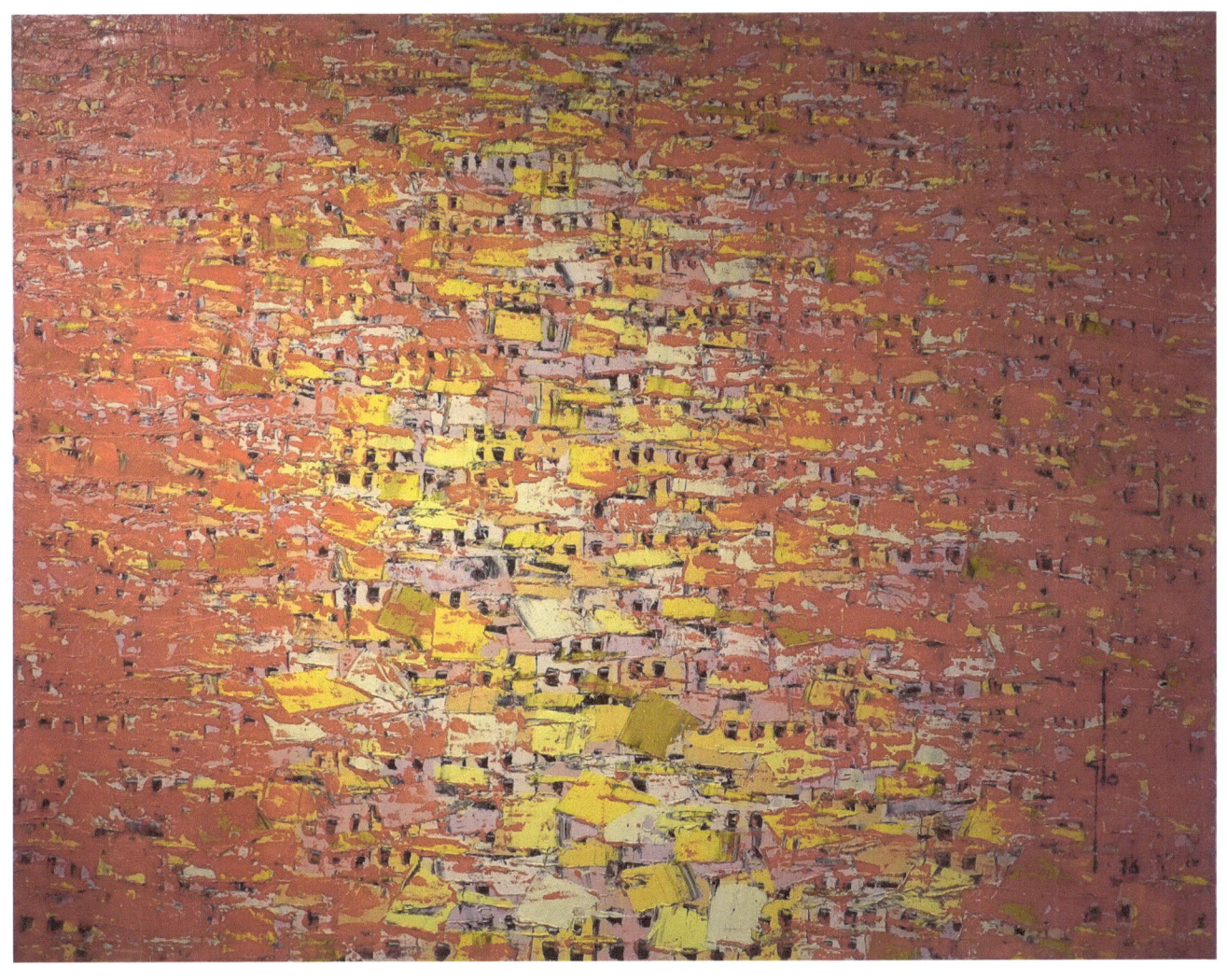

Red townscape, 2016, huile sur toile - 102 x 152 cm

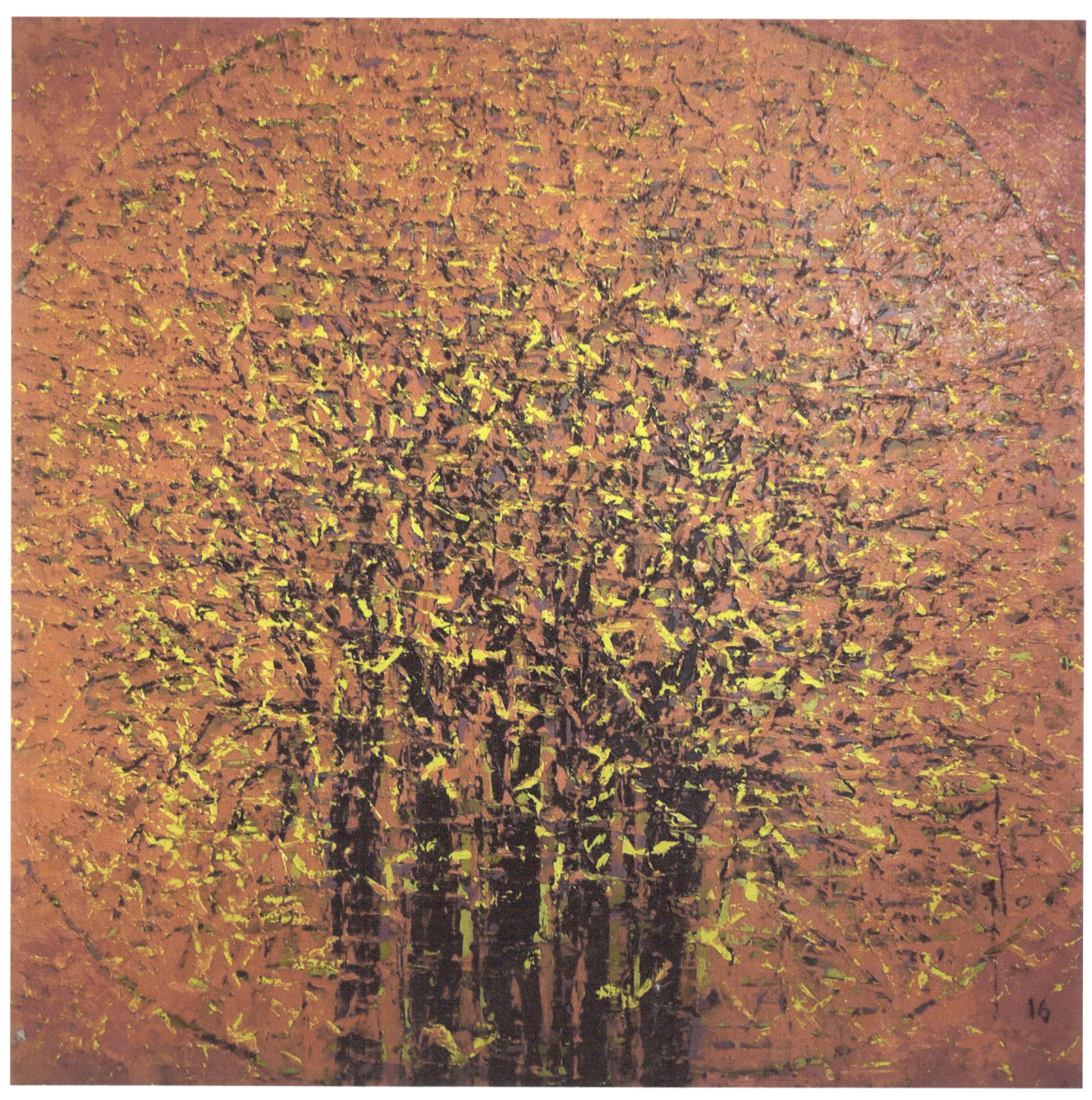

Red Forest - Bird Sanctuary, 2016, huile sur toile - 122 x 122 cm

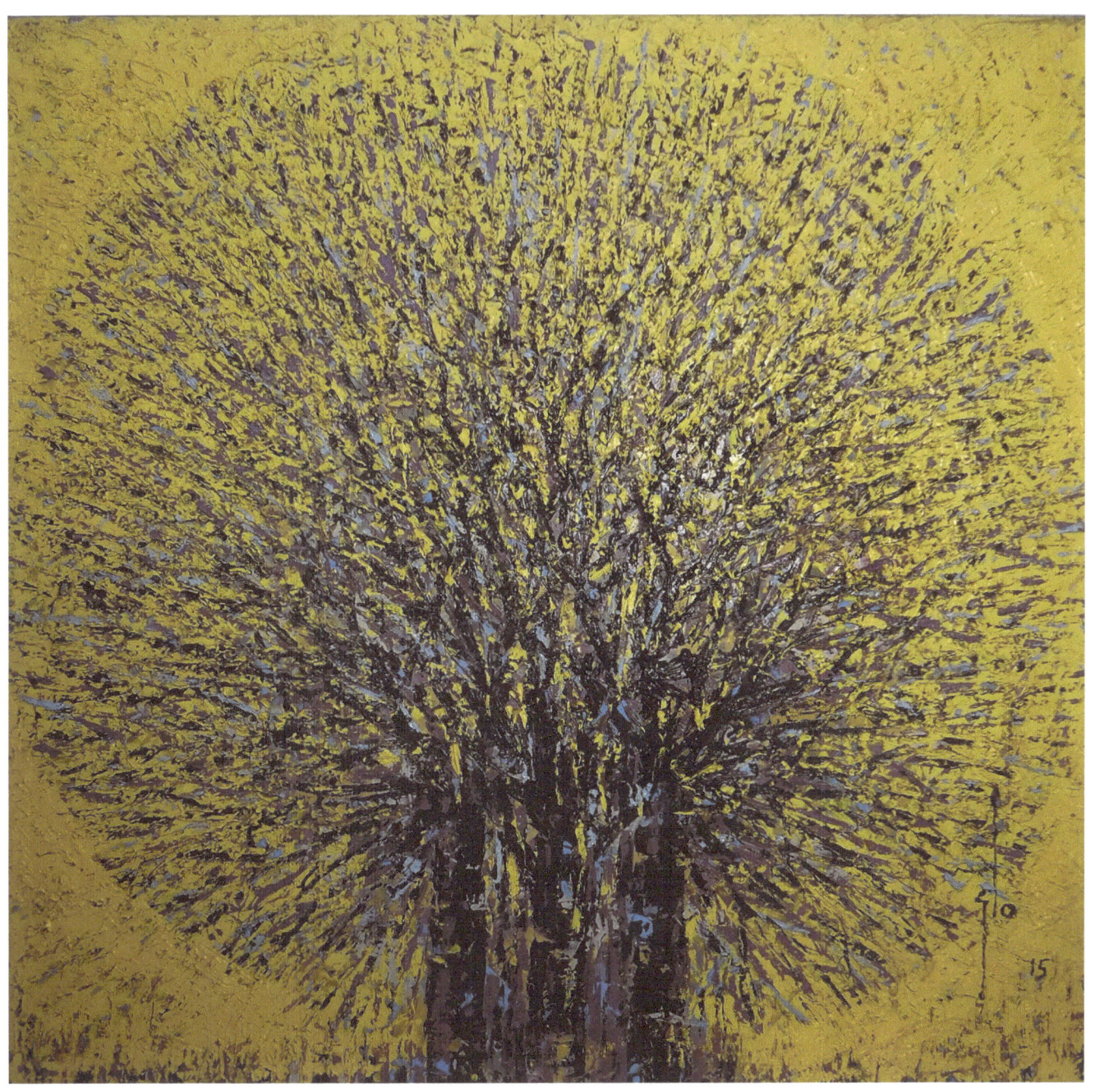

Yellow forest, 2015, huile sur toile - 122 x 122 cm

Bio

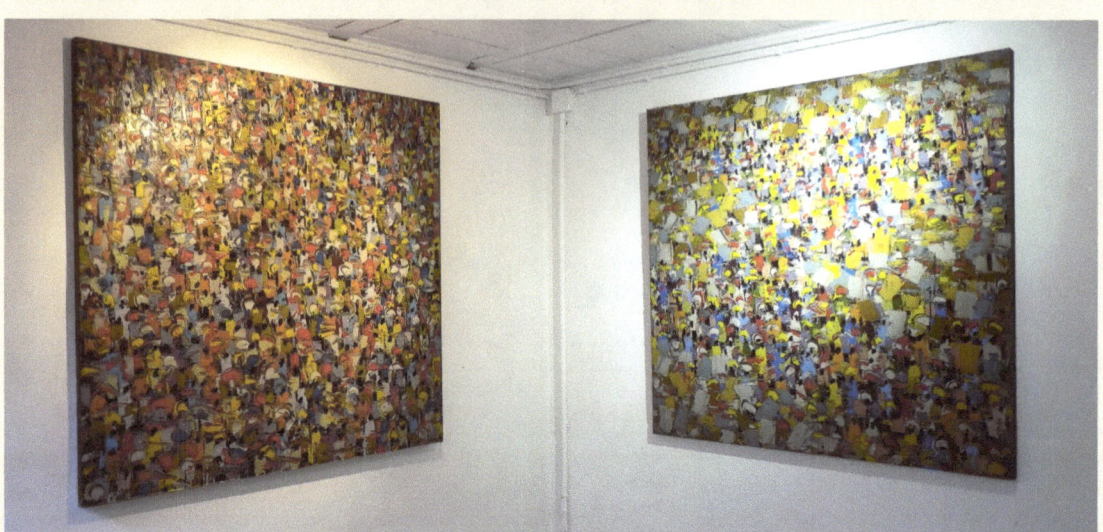

PROF. ABLADE GLOVER

Born in 1934, in Accra, Ghana, Ablade Glover has accumulated a number of distinctions, which underline his significance as an artist and enthusiastic educator both in Ghana and on the international art scene. The universality of Glover's work is reflected in the breadth and variety of his collectors. His work can be found in such diverse public and private collections around the world as the Dei Center in Accra, Ghana, the UNESCO Headquarters in Paris and Chicago's O'Hare International Airport amongst others. He has exhibited extensively in West Africa, Europe and the USA. A recipient of the distinguished AFGRAD Alumni Award by the African-American Institute in New York, he is a Life Fellow of the Royal Society of Art in London, as well as a fellow of the Ghana Academy of Arts and Sciences.

Prof. Ablade Glover completed his education (sometimes with scholarships from the Government of Ghana and US AID) at the following institutions:

- The Kumasi College of Technology (now Kwame Nkrumah University of Science and Technology), Ghana
- The Central School of Arts and Design (now University of the Arts London), London, UK
- Newcastle University, UK
- Kent State University, Kent Ohio, USA
- The Ohio State University, Columbus, Ohio, USA

After his educational studies, he settled down at the Kwame Nkrumah University of Science and Technology, where he taught for 30 years, rising from assistant lecturer to full professor. After retiring in 1994, he returned home to Accra and established the Artists Alliance Gallery, devoting his retirement years to the practices of African traditional and contemporary art.

Solo-shows (selected)

2015   Christopher Moller Gallery, Cape town

2014   October Gallery, London

2000   Galerie Arts Pluriels, Abidjan

Group show (selected)

2015   Africa Africans, Museu Afro Brazil, São Paulo, Brazil

2012   Transmission Part 2, Tasneem Gallery, Barcelona, Spain

COLLECTIONS (selected)

- AAI African American Institute Head Office, New York, USA
- Africa Centre, London, UK
- Afren art collection, London, UK
- Ashanti Goldfields Company Headquarters, Accra, Ghana
- Arts Council of Ghana, Accra, Ghana
- Barclays Bank Ghana Ltd., Accra, Ghana
- Commonwealth Foundation, London, UK
- Ghana Museums and Monuments Board, Accra, Ghana
- ICC International Conference Centre, Accra, Ghana
- Iris & B. Gerald Cantor Center for Visual Arts, Stanford University, California, USA
- Kosmos Energy, Texas, USA
- Mobil Oil Ghana Ltd., Accra, Ghana
- National Gallery of Modern Art, Lagos, Nigeria
- National Gallery of Zimbabwe, Harare, Zimbabwe
- O'Hare International Airport (mural), Chicago, USA
- Ohio State University International House, Columbus, USA
- Royal Collection of Prince and Princess Takamado, Tokyo, Japan
- Standard Chartered Bank Ghana Ltd., Accra, Ghana
- Tullow Oil PLC, London, UK
- UNESCO Headquarters, Paris, France
- Visiting Arts, London, UK
- World Bank, Washington DC, USA

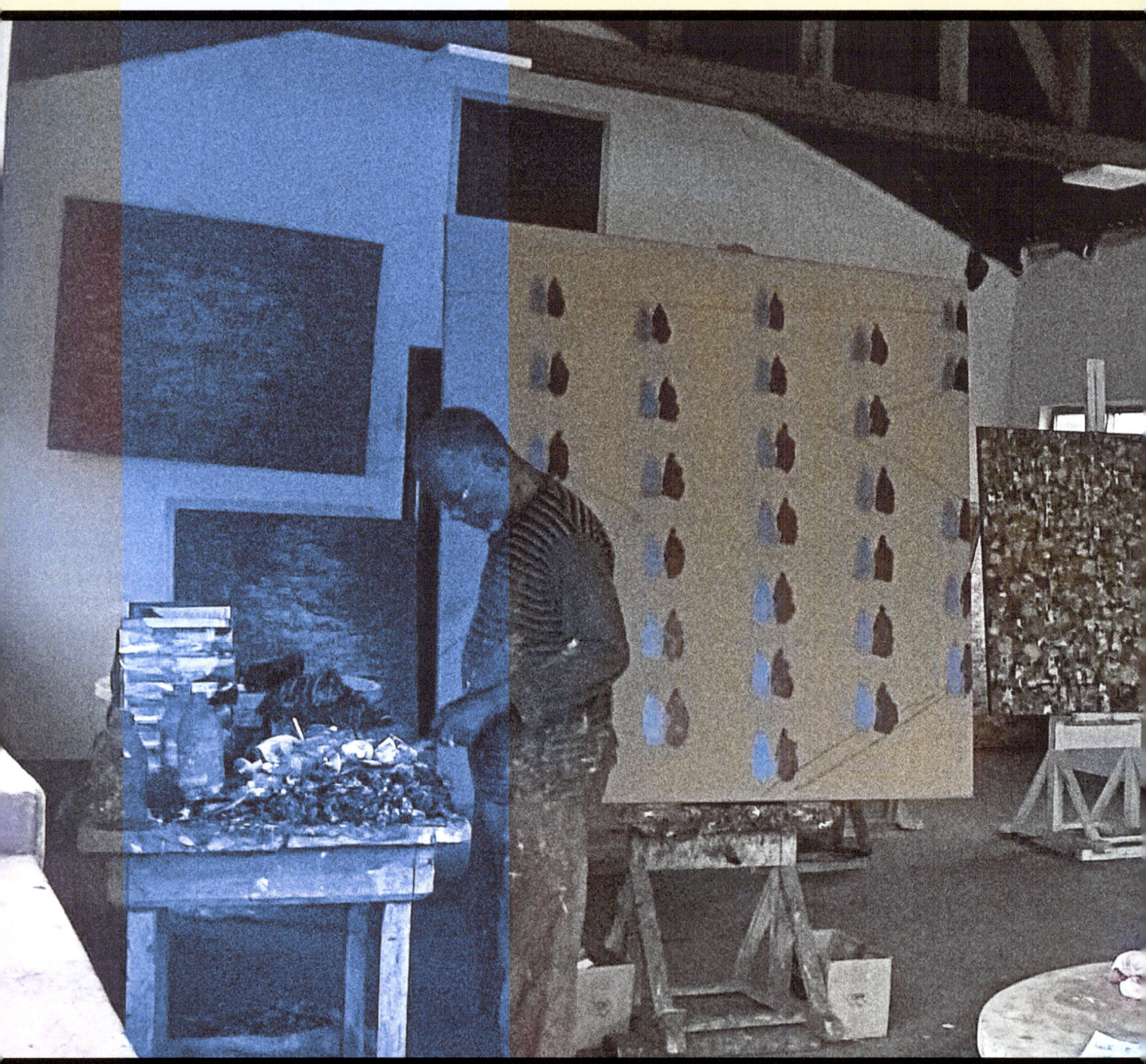

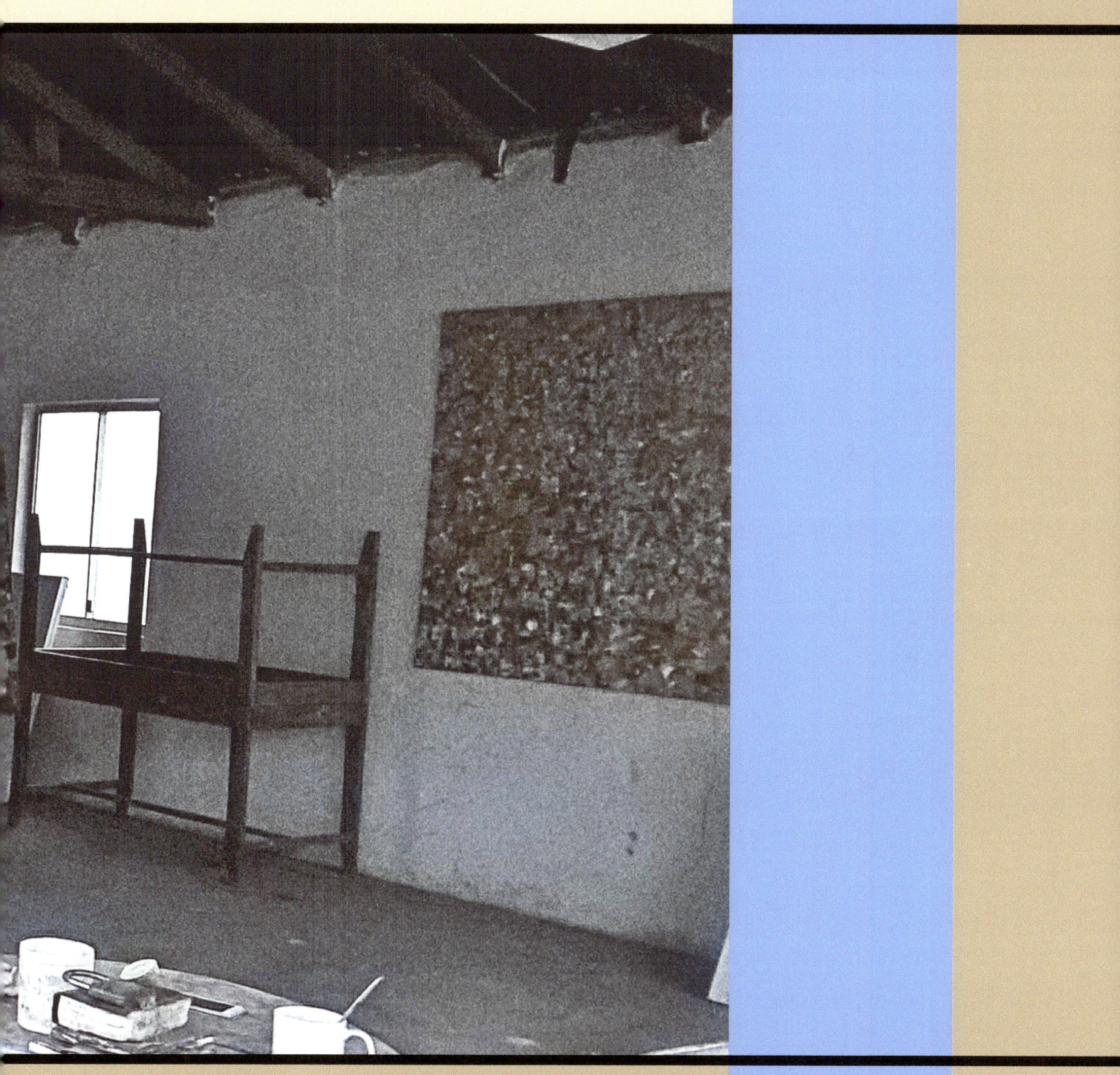

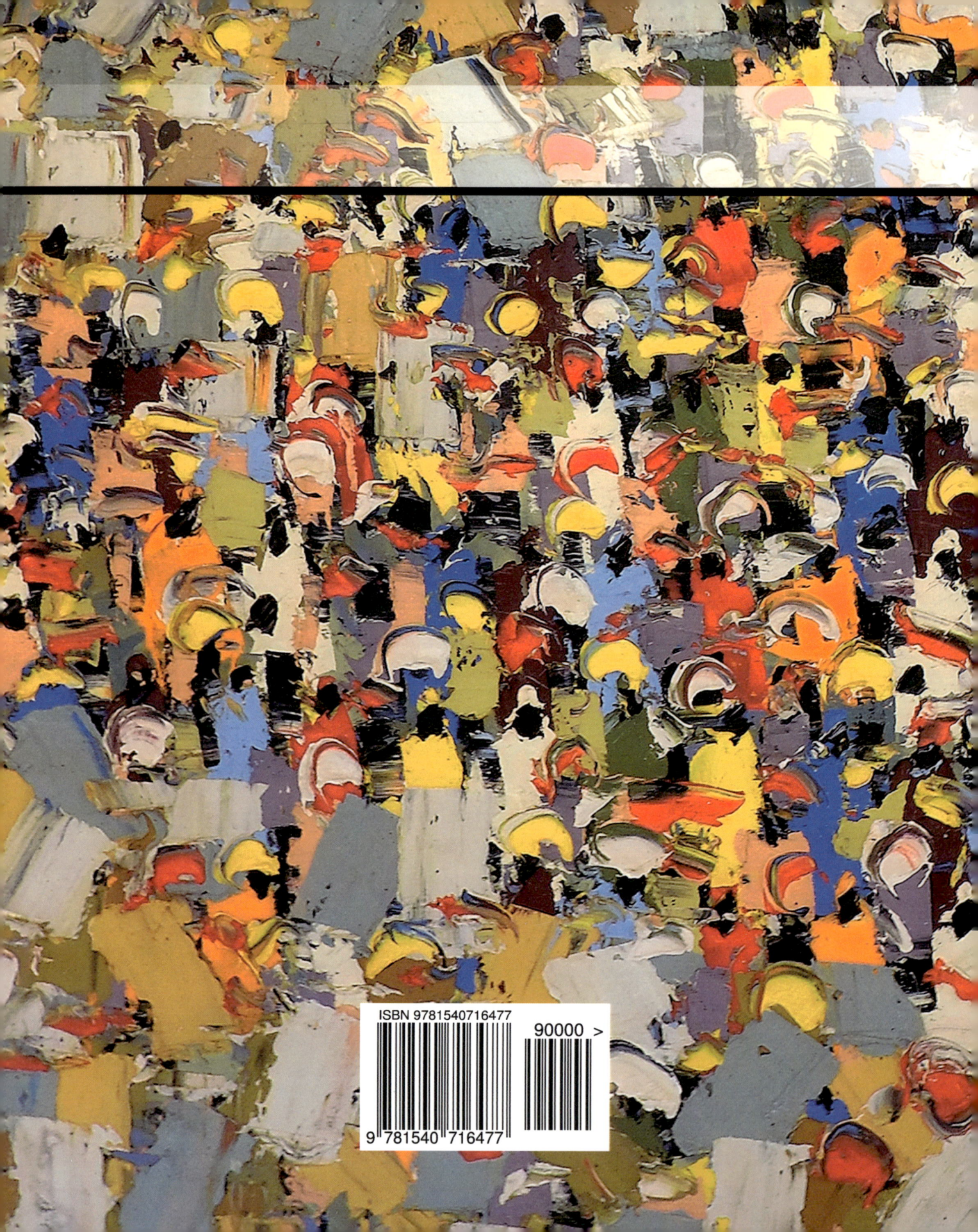

ISBN 9781540716477